THE TERRIBLE RAIN
The War Poets 1939–1945

This is a companion volume to Brian Gardner's anthology of the poetry of the First World War, *Up the Line to Death*. Many of the poets of the Second World War – at least forty of whom died on active service – are already forgotten. But here, too, are the poets whose fame has endured: Keith Douglas, Sidney Keyes, Alun Lewis and John Pudney; and the poets of the 'Home Front', such as Louis MacNeice and Dylan Thomas.

Over thirty years later these poems can be seen to be remarkable in their faithful recording of the spirit of their time. Anyone who remembers the Second World War will find in these pages the accurate and moving evocation of an age.

Also edited by Brian Gardner
(in Methuen Paperbacks)

UP THE LINE TO DEATH
The War Poets 1914–1918

THE TERRIBLE RAIN

The War Poets 1939–1945

AN ANTHOLOGY
selected and arranged, with
introduction and notes, by

BRIAN GARDNER

MAGNUM BOOKS
Methuen Paperbacks Ltd

A Magnum Book

THE TERRIBLE RAIN
0 417 02070 8

First published 1966 by Methuen & Co. Ltd
Magnum edition published 1977
This anthology © 1966 by Brian Gardner

Magnum Books are published by
Methuen Paperbacks Ltd
11 New Fetter Lane, London EC4P 4EE

Made and printed in Great Britain by
Hazell Watson & Viney Ltd, Aylesbury, Bucks

CONTENTS

When No Allies Are Left

The Blazing Fire

CONTENTS

The Desert

The Cruel Sea

Home Front

Beneath The German Sky

Brief Encounter

After Several Years

The Jungle

Into Europe

Victory

CONTENTS

ACKNOWLEDGEMENTS

The editor and publishers wish to thank the following for permission to reproduce the poems listed below:

Kenneth Allott for a poem from *The Ventriloquist's Doll* (The Cresset Press); The Favil Press Ltd for poems by Brian Allwood from *Resurgam 10*; Walter Andrewes for a poem from *Penguin New Writing* (Penguin Books); John Arlott for a poem from *Clausentum* (Jonathan Cape); W. H. Auden for poems from *Collected Shorter Poems* (Faber & Faber); Bruce Bain for poems from *Poets Now 2* (Favil Press); Peter Baker for a poem from *Resurgam I* (Favil Press); Michael Barsley for a poem from *Horizon*; George Barker for a poem from *Personal Sonnets* (Faber & Faber); John Bayliss for a poem from *The White Knight* (Fortune Press); D. van den Bogaerde for a poem from *Poetry Review*; The Bodley Head Ltd for a poem by David Bourne from *Poems*; Communist Party of Great Britain for an untitled poem by Clive Branson from *British Soldier in India*; Dr J. Bronowski for a poem from *Penguin New Writing* (Penguin Books); Jocelyn Brooke for a poem from *December Spring* (The Bodley Head); John Buxton for a poem from *Such Liberty* (Macmillan); The Hogarth Press for poems by Norman Cameron from *Collected Poems*; The Bodley Head Ltd for a poem by Roy Campbell from *Collected Poems Vol II*; James K. Cassels for a poem from *Poems From India* (Oxford University Press, India); Charles Causley for poems from *Union Street* and *Survivor's Leave* (Rupert Hart-Davis); Robert L. Chaloner for a poem from *More Poems From the Forces* (Routledge & Kegan Paul); Macmillan & Co Ltd and the Macmillan Company of Canada Ltd for a poem by Robert Conquest from *Poems*; Herbert Corby for three poems from *Hampdens Going Over* (Nicholson & Watson); the Executors of the John Cornford Estate for a poem from *A Memoir* (Jonathan Cape); R. N. Currey for poems from *This Other Planet* (Routledge &

Kegan Paul); Paul Dehn for poems from *The Day's Alarm* (Hamish Hamilton); Methuen & Co Ltd for a poem by Patric Dickinson from *Stone in the Midst*; Mrs Marie J. Douglas for poems by Keith Douglas from *Selected Poems* (Faber & Faber); Gavin Ewart for poems from *Horizon*, *More Poems From the Forces* (Routledge & Kegan Paul) and *Poetry From Cambridge in Wartime* (Fortune Press); the joint copyright holders of *The Unreturning Spring* by James Farrar, Mrs Margaret Farrar and Henry Williamson; Mrs E. B. Moore for Keith Foottit's poem, which appeared in *For Your Tomorrow* (Oxford University Press); G. S. Fraser for poems from *Home Town Elegy* (Poetry London, 1944); David Gascoyne for a poem from *Collected Poems* (Oxford University Press); John Gawsworth for a poem from *Collected Poems* (Sidgwick & Jackson); Bernard Gutteridge for poems from *Traveller's Eye* (Routledge & Kegan Paul); the Executors of the Estate of Stephan Haggard for poems from *I'll Go to Bed at Noon* (Faber & Faber); Charles Hamblett for a poem from *Poems From the Forces* (Routledge & Kegan Paul); Michael Hamburger for a poem from *Flowering Cactus* (Hand & Flower Press); Norman Hampson for a poem from *More Poems From the Forces* (Routledge & Kegan Paul), and for a poem from *Penguin New Writing* (Penguin Books); Arthur Barker Ltd for a poem by Christopher Hassall from *The Slow Nights*; Hamish Henderson for a poem from *Elegies for the Dead* (John Lehmann); Rayner Heppenstall for a poem from *Poems* (Martin Secker & Warburg); Routledge & Kegan Paul Ltd for a poem by T. R. Hodgson from *This Life, This Death*; A. M. Heath & Company Ltd for a poem by John Jarmain from *Poems*; Mrs E. B. Moore for a poem by D. Geraint Jones from *For Your Tomorrow* (Oxford University Press); Routledge & Kegan Paul Ltd for poems by Sidney Keyes from *Collected Poems*; Francis King for a poem from *Rod of Incantation* (Longmans, Green); Patricia Ledward for a poem from *Poems of This War* (Cambridge University Press); Laurie Lee for a poem from *The Sun My Monument* (The Hogarth Press); John Lehmann for a poem from *Collected Poems* (Eyre & Spottiswoode); George Allen & Unwin Ltd for poems by Alun

Lewis from *Raiders Dawn* and *Ha Ha Among the Trumpets*; C. Day Lewis for a poem from *Word Over All* (Jonathan Cape); Jack Lindsay for a poem from *New Lyrical Ballads* (Poetry London); Maurice Lindsay for a poem from *Sailing Tomorrow's Seas* (Fortune Press); Lawrence Little for a poem from *Penguin New Writing* (Penguin Books); Emanuel Litvinoff for a poem from *Poets Now Series* (Favil Press); Faber & Faber Ltd for poems by Louis MacNeice from *Autumn Journal* and *Collected Poems*; H. B. Mallalieu for poems from *More Poems From the Forces* (Routledge & Kegan Paul); John Manifold for a poem from *Selected Verse* Copyright © 1946 by John Manifold by permission of The John Day Company Inc; Hubert Nicholson for a poem from *New Lyrical Ballads* (Poetry London); Norman Nicholson for a poem from *Five Rivers* (Faber & Faber); William Plomer for a poem from *Collected Poems* (Jonathan Cape); Alex Potter for a poem from *Verses by British Internees*; The Rt Hon Enoch Powell for a poem from *Dancer's End* (Falcon Press); F. T. Prince for a poem from *The Doors of Stone* (Rupert Hart-Davis); John Pudney for poems from *Collected Poems* (Putnam); the Misses V. and E. Ramsey for an extract from *Poems of the War Years* (Macmillan); Derek B. Reade for a poem from *Poetry Review*; Henry Reed for poems from *A Map of Verona* (Jonathan Cape); Keidrych Rhys for a poem from *Wales*; Michael Riviere for a poem from *Penguin New Writing* (Penguin Books); Anne Ridler for a poem from *The Nine Bright Shiners* (Faber & Faber); Alan Rook for a poem from *Soldiers, This Solitude* (Routledge & Kegan Paul); Alan Ross for poems from *Something of the Sea* (Derek Verschoyle); Patrick Savage for a poem from *Home is the Soldier* (Fortune Press); David Higham Associates for a poem by Dorothy L. Sayers published in the *Times Literary Supplement*; Vernon Scannell for a poem from *Forty Poems and Ballads* (Eyre & Spottiswoode); Francis Scarfe for a poem from *Forty Poems and Ballads* (Eyre & Spottiswoode); Paul Scott for a poem from *Poets Now Series* (Favil Press); Ian Serraillier for a poem from *Poems of This War* (Oxford University Press); the Executors of Dame Edith Sitwell for a poem from *Collected Poems* (Macmillan);

Martyn Skinner for a poem from *Letters to Malaya* (Putnam); Sidgwick & Jackson Ltd for a poem by Richard Spender from *The Collected Poems of Richard Spender*; Stephen Spender for poems from *Collected Poems* (Faber & Faber); Derek Stanford for a poem from *Music for Statues* (Routledge & Kegan Paul); Gordon Swaine for a poem from *More Poems From the Forces* (Routledge & Kegan Paul); Julian Symons for a poem from *The Second Man* (Routledge & Kegan Paul); George Taylor for a poem from *Poems From India* (Oxford University Press, India); Hubert Nicholson, Literary Executor for A. S. J. Tessimond, for a poem from *Voices in a Giant City* (William Heinemann); the Literary Executors of the Dylan Thomas Estate for a poem from *Deaths and Entrances* (J. M. Dent & Sons); Victor Gollancz Ltd for a poem by Frank Thompson from *There is a Spirit in Europe*; Terence Tiller for a poem from *Unarm, Eros* (The Hogarth Press); Ruthven Todd for a poem from *These Are Facts* (J. M. Dent & Sons); Henry Treece for poems from *The Black Seasons* (Faber & Faber); Geoffrey A. Wagner for a poem published by The Fortune Press; James Walker for an extract from *Poems of the War Years* (Macmillan); Sir John Waller for poems from *Horizon* and *The Kiss of Stars* (William Heinemann); John Wedge for a poem from *More Poems From the Forces* (Routledge & Kegan Paul); University of Texas for a poem by Denton Welch from *A Last Sheaf* (John Lehmann); Faber & Faber Ltd for a poem by Nigel Weir from *Verses of a Fighter Pilot* (Faber & Faber); L. J. Yates for a poem from *New Writing and Daylight* (The Hogarth Press); Geoffrey Matthews for a poem from *New Lyrical Ballads* (Nicholson and Watson).

Every effort has been made to trace copyright holders, but in some cases they could not be found. The editor and publishers wish to apologize for consequent omissions.

INTRODUCTORY NOTE

One hundred and nineteen poets of the Second World War are in this book. Of them almost one in six were silenced in that conflict: a conflict close at hand in the scale of history, but now accelerating away fast into distant memory.

Many types of poem are here, but all are chosen because they seemed to express genuine and relevant attitudes to the war. I have tried to capture something of the flavour, as well as of the best poetry, of 1939–45. This, I hope, has excused me from a too-slavish respect for reputations, and allowed the inclusion of some lesser-known and forgotten poets; also, of some poetry of lesser quality perhaps that is valid in the context.

It is possible to detect some definite streams. The eldest poets in this book were those whose reputations and attitudes were forged in the nineteen-thirties; some discipline on the size of the book being necessary, with but three exceptions I have reached back no further than their generation. They came to the war with few if any illusions, acute political and social consciousness, incisive techniques, and popular vocabularies. They were well equipped to write the poetry of Hitler's war, but before long they seemed already to belong to the inter-war age. Into the war beside the 'Auden group' went the New Apocalyptics, the surrealists, the blatant obscurantists, the neo-Georgians, and individualists of Geoffrey Grigson's *New Verse*.

But the privacies of the nineteen-thirties' poets, for ever writing and dedicating poetry to each other, and their exclusive if bitter squabbling, were left to the past. At first, contrary to a popular idea, there was a considerable wave of patriotic, neo-Brookean verse in most, if not all, of the poetry publications. I have left most of this undisturbed, as it was not symptomatic of a general mood, and most of it was not distinguished as poetry.

In the first year of war, the newspapers, no doubt searching for some dramatic Rupert Brooke-like figure on whom to peg stories, asked in some dudgeon: Where Are the War Poets? Cyril Connolly, and then Keidrych Rhys, answered: Under Your Nose.* But the newspapers, as is their immemorial wont, preferred to answer their own questions themselves. They answered: Ran away. Auden and MacNeice, on peaceful academic business in America, shortly joined by George Barker from Japan, found themselves in the full glare of British disapproval. There was a mood reminiscent of the more extreme and unlovely 'white feather' hysteria of the First War. The question was repeated in Parliament. MacNeice came home. Auden gave assurances of loyalty. The newspapers turned to other controversies. But having discovered where *some* of the poets were, the question remained: where was the poetry?

It became evident that perhaps Rhys had been right after all. For in two anthologies he once more gave a splendid answer. Rhys's two books were not only comprehensive, they paid no attention to the pre-war cliques that from time to time bedevilled other anthologists and editors. This was a war even better served by editors than by poets. Over a dozen sympathetic and dedicated editors replaced their only two important equivalents of the First War. John Lehmann's *Penguin New Writing* and Cyril Connolly's *Horizon* would have been outstanding publications at any time; when European civilization suddenly seemed about as dead as the Romans they were invaluable.

By 1941 a remarkable thing had happened. From poetry being the almost private game of a literary set, which, despite Auden's efforts to disentangle it from the Sitwell web of the public's imagination, it had sometimes seemed to be – there came something like a people's poetry. 'Leave this book at a Post Office when you have read it, so that men and women in the services may enjoy it too,' was the advice of *New Writing*.

* And, also in answer to the Press, Day Lewis was to write his terse 'Where Are the War Poets?' But Stevie Smith wrote, in 'The Poets Are Silent', that the poets ought to remain silent about the war.

> And we stretched out, unbuttoning our braces,
> Smoking a Woodbine, darning dirty socks,
> Reading the Sunday papers – I saw a fox.

So wrote Alun Lewis. It was something everyone who was experiencing service life could share. Magazines of poetry and short stories sold in their thousands to troops waiting for trains in 'dimmed-out' stations. Hundreds and thousands of men and women in the forces read and enjoyed poetry for the first, and last, time. Not always without difficulty; 'A Soldier's Soliloquy' was printed in *Poetry Review* thus:

> It's quiet, very quiet, here in the olive groves,
> With only the distant drone of a plane beyond [*censored*],
> Or the ceaseless grinding of the grasshoppers in the trees.

By 1944 one of the best-selling books was an anthology of poetry; an anthology, moreover, that was edited by one of the war's leading generals. It was even suggested, by Herbert Read, that there should be official war poets as well as war artists; and H. E. Bates – who wrote war poetry as well – was officially commissioned to write the stories of 'Flying Officer X'.

It was a time when 'remember' was rhymed with 'Stavanger', 'gardens' with 'air-raid wardens', and, more felicitous:

> The draggled flowers and the broken vases
> And Churchill shouting insults at the Nazis.*

A new style emerged: nonchalant, cool, laconic. It was not only evident in the poetry of men like Walter Andrewes, Norman Cameron, R. N. Currey, and Gavin Ewart, but also in the short stories of the time, particularly those of J. Maclaren-Ross. Antiheroics were popular, although the R.A.F. poets were never quite a part of this mood; but even Timothy Corsellis's fighter pilots were drawn together, not by some crusade, but 'by a common love of pornography and the desire to outdrink one another'.

* 'Pence To The Pound', T. W. Ramsey.

However, the opposite trend was also, inevitably, present. If you want to say something in poetry, but think that you may well die in battle at any moment, there is an obvious danger of over-reaching. Such a spur brought forth from Wilfred Owen the greatest war poems in the English language. But it may be that Sidney Keyes and Alun Lewis, the two most often mentioned as the Second World War's greatest poets, over-reached themselves in what is considered to be their most important work. Keyes, in fact, wrote rather little war poetry that has survived (he is believed to have had some on his person at his death), although his 'Expected Guest' is a major achievement. Alun Lewis was devoting himself more and more to the short story. Keith Douglas, perhaps, comes nearest to Owen, and is the outstanding poet of battle to come out of the war. If until recently he has been comparatively neglected, perhaps it is because in the past anthologists have tended to reproduce his more ambitious, philosophic, and difficult 'base-area' poems, and have neglected the easier but powerful poems of the front line. (Douglas probably saw more of battle than even Owen himself.) These three poets were all conscious of their First War predecessors, particularly Lewis of Edward Thomas, and Douglas of Isaac Rosenberg. The influence of Siegfried Sassoon can be seen on Kenneth Neal, John Wedge, and, a poet not represented here, Michael Savage. But the First War poet who seems closest to many of those of the following war is Edmund Blunden, who had spoken with their kind of under-statement.

Premature death, particularly in battle, can do great things for the reputation of a poet. Those who survive – or many of them – become 'poets' rather than 'war poets'. But Louis MacNeice, Roy Fuller and Alan Rook, for instance, wrote more consistently good war poems than did nearly all of those who died added together. Nevertheless, some of those who died have been – unjustly so it seems to me – virtually forgotten.

At first, it seemed that Stephen Haggard was to be recommended to posterity as the war's famous poet. In 1944, his work received the extraordinary compliment of two full-page articles, in successive issues, in *The Times Literary Supplement*. But in the following year the outstanding poets lost in the war were named in the same august journal as: Keith Douglas, Sidney Keyes, Alun Lewis, Richard Spender. Haggard's reputation rapidly, and no doubt justly, declined. But are we sure that others have not the quality to survive?

Despite the much greater overall death-rate in the First World War, I believe more published poets died in the Second; and when one adds to them such names as Richard Hillary,* Rex Whistler, and Rollo Woolley, the loss of talent has been hard enough. And certainly the non-commissioned servicemen were far better represented among the poets of the Second War.

It was total war: many a civilian – including the young – had a greater experience of the tensions, horrors, and disciplines of 'battle' than the majority of servicemen. For this reason the ordeal by Blitz, for instance, is well represented here.

What had begun with an air of subdued excitement and a kind of relief, ended with weariness. By the end of a long war, a new generation of poets, who had not experienced the conflicts of the thirties, had come on the scene; Francis King, Alan Ross, Vernon Scannell ... they had been schoolboys during the years when their elders had been drawn by the Communist magnet. Their maturity had been forged not in the Spanish Civil War but in the Second World War. The age of Chamberlain's umbrella was more like sixteen than six years from the age of the mushroom cloud. Squashed uncomfortably between these two groups was the immediate pre-war set at Oxford and Cambridge and their counterparts at the other universities: an active group of poets led by men like John Heath-Stubbs, Nicholas Moore, and Michael Meyer – and from whom Douglas, Keyes, and Drummond Allison sprung. It was these *literati* who, it was expected, would be the leaders of a post-Auden era.

The war was the meeting-ground of these generations of poets. Many of the poets of the nineteen-thirties, while having few illusions, thought in 1939 that the war's end might indeed herald

---

* Hillary, I believe, wrote some poetry, but his father writes: 'As far as I know Richard never wrote any verse that he would have wished published.'

some golden – or at any rate silver – age, some 'new deal' in
Europe. Dorothy L. Sayers had hoped for:

> Some sense, some decency, perhaps
> Some justice, too, if we are able,
> With no sly jackals round our table.

But when the time came, Francis King bleakly noted:

> Our three old landlords sit and quarrel,
> For a dead rose
> And a few sheaves of thistle, rue and sorrel.

That 1945 heralded history's most cruel and bitter peace was not
a cause for jubilation. The poets knew this, accepted it.

The book is arranged in an attempt to reveal a particular period
of history. It is hoped that it will be read from the beginning through
to the end.

I have not confined myself strictly to poetry written between late
1939 and August 1945. MacNeice's 'Meeting Point', for example,
was written just before the start of war, but not only was it perhaps
the best love poem of the time, it also seems to belong in these pages.

I have ended with two extracts from 'The Shadow of Cain', not
because the war ended with a particularly religious mood, but be-
cause Edith Sitwell's was one of the few attempts to write a major
poem about a supremely major event. Hiroshima was, as well, an
occurrence to which most people must have had a deeply personal
reaction. Edith Sitwell may not have been widely accepted by the
pre-war generation of poets, but she did have courage. Although
there are some exceptions, it is perhaps disappointing that more
poets did not accept the challenge to respond, in poetic terms, to
Hiroshima. Auden's notable 'Age of Anxiety', however, cannot pass
without mention.*

The First War produced the greater poetry: but there is a great

* Nor 'The Trumpet of Hiroshima' by Patric Dickinson. Nor, indeed, the
achievement of Thomas Thorneley: 'The Atom', published in 1939, in which
he predicted the event

deal more good poetry of the Second War; so much so as to provide grave embarrassment to the anthologist. Unlike in a previous anthology, of the First World War, I have had to exclude the American poets. (The British poets of the war created some interest in the United States. *The New Republic* published an anthology, and there were at least two splendid anthologies by Oscar Williams, containing British poets like Corsellis and Mallalieu.)

Collections could have been produced on the Blitz, on the Desert, alone.

Notable poems missing from these pages include: 'Triumphal Ode, 1939' by George Barker; 'In Westminster Abbey' by John Betjeman; 'Dead Men' by Keith Douglas; 'The Divided Ways' by John Heath-Stubbs; 'The Sphere of Glass' by John Lehmann; 'Postscript, For Gweno' by Alun Lewis; 'Signals Section' by Lawrence Little; 'Aftermath' by Louis MacNeice; 'Reading in War Time' by Edwin Muir; 'The Question' by F. T. Prince; 'At Parting' by Anne Ridler; 'Dunkirk Pier' by Alan Rook; 'September Holiday, 1939' by Clive Sansom; 'On the Death of Alun Lewis' by Vernon Watkins; and poems by N. K. Cruickshank, W. S. Graham, J. C. Hall and many others.

Lesser-known poems for which I should like to have found room included, most particularly, 'Into The Greeness' by R. Brian Scott, the young poet who died in the Tunisian campaign: and also, 'The Last War' by Kingsley Amis; 'War' by Jock Curle; 'Back to Billet' by G. Eades; 'Cigarette for the Bambino' by Gavin Ewart; 'The Bomber' by B. R. Gibbs; 'Backward Look' by Valentin Iremonger; 'Conscript' by Philip Larkin; 'Over the Water' by Patrick Mac-Donagh; 'Twenty-Four Hours Leave' by Alan Pryce-Jones;

> Wake not the imprisoned power that sleeps
> Unknown, or dimly guessed, in thee . . .
> Keep those grim forces buried deep,
> That in thine atoms repose.

and 'Presage', published in October 1945, a poem in which he wrote on the event of the first atomic bombing.

'Hymn Without Choir or Organ' by Derek Stanford; 'Patriotic Poem' by John Wain; 'No Use Pretending' by Robert Waller; and 'American Games' by Demetrios Capetanikis.

For Laurence Whistler's 'In The Fog' I was unable to obtain the author's permission; and Roy Fuller – a very sad loss – would not agree to my selection, feeling it unrepresentative of his best, and declined an invitation to make his own.

As part of my purpose has been to recapture something of the essence of the war, I could not, I hope, be expected to include those poems which penetrated exclusively into the poet's mind, rather than studied the lie of the human land around them, technically excellent as they may have been. Those poets given to excess of obscurity were not, I imagine, primarily concerned with communication anyway. On this subject, one of the war poets, John Bayliss, wrote in 1944: 'I hold that it is not the business of the poet deliberately to mystify . . . because I wish to make some attempt to reach a wider public than a few intellectuals. Probably this is too optimistic, but I believe it is worth the attempt.'

I am grateful to many poets in the book and out of it for offering and giving various kinds of help; and especially to John Bayliss, Maurice Lindsay, and Sir John Waller. My thanks go once again to John D. Cullen for publishing poetry at all; and to Miss Dominie Bertelli and Mrs Ann Cazalet for much work in copyright research. And finally I thank the poets themselves, or the heirs of the poets, for their trust.

War is, without doubt, man's most outrageous activity, and yet it draws from him, too, nobility, valour, and art. Here is some of the poetry which came from what was, after all, the only necessary war of modern history . . . with its alternating periods of danger and boredom, its resignation, its sense of communal courage, and its essential honesty. A time of war; not any war, but, like all such, one of special flavour to the memory of those fortunate enough to have survived it. A time of railway stations awash with uniforms, of cardboard windows and blank signposts, of the nine o'clock news with some-one reading it, of previously exotic jungles and unheard-of deserts, of some of our aircraft reported missing, of the lingering scent of explosive, of blue-pencilled letters, of car-headlamp masks, of bombers' moons, of wishing luck as you waved goodbye, and of poetry.

B. G.

Prelude

Full Moon At Tierz:
Before The Storming Of Huesca

I

The past, a glacier, gripped the mountain wall,
And time was inches, dark was all.
But here it scales the end of the range,
The dialectic's point of change,
Crashes in light and minutes to its fall.

Time present is a cataract whose force
Breaks down the banks even at its source
And history forming in our hand's
Not plasticine but roaring sands,
Yet we must swing it to its final course.

The intersecting lines that cross both ways,
Time future, has no image in space,
Crooked as the road that we must tread,
Straight as our bullets fly ahead.
We are the future. The last fight let us face.

JOHN CORNFORD
killed in action, Cordoba, 1936

Yes, We Are Going To Suffer

Yes, We Are Going To Suffer

Yes, we are going to suffer, now; the sky
Throbs like a feverish forehead; pain is real;
The groping searchlights suddenly reveal
The little natures that will make us cry,

Who never quite believed they could exist,
Not where we were. They take us by surprise
Like ugly long-forgotten memories,
And like a conscience all the guns resist.

Behind each sociable home-loving eye
The private massacres are taking place;
All women, Jews, the Rich, the Human Race.

The mountains cannot judge us when we lie:
We dwell upon the earth; the earth obeys
The intelligent and evil till they die.

W. H. AUDEN

England

Plush bees above a bed of dahlias;
  Leisurely, timeless garden teas;
Brown bread and honey; scent of mowing;
  The still green light below tall trees.

The ancient custom of deception;
  A Press that seldom stoops to lies –
Merely suppresses truth and twists it,
  Blandly corrupt and slyly wise.

The Common Man; his mask of laughter;
    His back-chat while the roof falls in;
Minorities' long losing battles
    Fought that the sons of sons may win.

The politician's inward snigger
    (Big business on the private phone);
The knack of sitting snug on fences;
    The double face of flesh and stone.

Grape-bloom of distant woods at dusk;
    Storm-crown on Glaramara's head;
The fire-rose over London night;
    An old plough rusting autumn-red.

The 'incorruptible policeman'
    Gaoling the whore whose bribe's run out,
Guarding the rich against the poor man,
    Guarding the Settled Gods from doubt.

The generous smile of music-halls,
    Bars and bank-holidays and queues;
The private peace of public foes;
    The truce of pipe and football news.

The smile of privilege exultant;
    Smile at the 'bloody Red' defeated;
Smile at the striker starved and broken;
    Smile at the 'dirty nigger' cheated.

The old hereditary craftsman;
    The incommunicable skill;
The pride in long-loved tools, refusal
    To do the set job quick or ill.

The greater artist mocked, misflattered;
  The lesser forming clique and team,
Or crouching in his narrow corner,
  Narcissus with his secret dream.

England of rebels – Blake and Shelley;
  England where freedom's sometimes won,
Where Jew and Negro needn't fear yet
  Lynch-law and pogrom, whip and gun.

England of cant and smug discretion;
  England of wagecut-sweatshop-knight,
Of sportsman-churchman-slum-exploiter,
  Of puritan grown sour with spite.

England of clever fool, mad genius,
  Timorous lion and arrogant sheep,
Half-hearted snob and shamefaced bully,
  Of hands that wake and eyes that sleep . . .
England the snail that's shod with lightning . . .
  Shall we laugh or shall we weep?

                           A. S. J. TESSIMOND
                           Autumn 1938

Father And Son: 1939

A family portrait not too stale to record
Of a pleasant old buffer, nephew to a lord,
Who believed that the bank was mightier than the sword,
And that an umbrella might pacify barbarians abroad:
              Just like an old liberal
              Between the wars.

With an easy existence, and a cosy country place,
And with hardly a wrinkle, at sixty, in his face,
Growing old with old books, with old wine, and with grace,
Unaware that events move with breakneck pace:
                    Just like an old diehard
                    Between the wars.

With innocuous tastes in common with his mate,
A love of his garden and his tidy snug estate,
Of dogs, music and children, and lying in bed late,
And no disposition to quarrel with his fate:
                    Just like an old Englishman
                    Between the wars.

With no religion or imagination, and a hazy lazy view
Of the great world where trouble kept cropping up anew,
With old clubmen for friends, who would seem stuffy to you,
Old faded prigs, but gentlemen (give them their due):
                    Just like an old fossil
                    Between the wars.

With a kindly old wife who subscribed for the oppressed,
With an O.B.E., and a hair-do like a last year's bird's nest,
Even more tolerant than anyone would have guessed,
Who hoped that in the long run all was for the best:
                    Just like an old lady
                    Between the wars.

With one child, a son, who in spite of his education
Showed only a modicum of common sense or cultivation,
Sometimes read the *Daily Worker* or the *New Statesman and Nation*,
But neither, it must be admitted, with much concentration:
                    Just like a young playboy
                    Between the wars.

With a firm grasp of half-truths, with political short-sight,
With a belief we could disarm but at the same time fight,
And that only the Left Wing could ever be right,
And that Moscow, of all places, was the sole source of light:
> Just like a young hopeful
> Between the wars.

With a flash flat in Chelsea of a bogus elegance,
With surrealist pictures and books puffed by Gollancz,
With a degree of complacence which nothing could enhance,
And without one sole well-wisher to kick him in the pants:
> Just like a young smarty
> Between the wars.

With a precious mistress who thought she could paint
But could neither show respect nor exercise restraint,
Was a perfect goose-cap, and thought good manners quaint,
With affectation enough to try the patience of a saint:
> Just like a young cutie
> Between the wars.

With a succession of parties for sponges and bores,
With a traffic-jam outside (for they turned up in scores),
With first-rate sherry flowing into second-rate whores,
And third-rate conversation without one single pause:
> Just like a young couple
> Between the wars.

With weekends in the country and holidays in France,
With promiscuous habits, time to sunbathe and dance,
And even to write books that were hardly worth a glance,
Earning neither reputation nor publisher's advance:
> Just like a young writer
> Between the wars.

On a Sunday in September other troubles had begun,
There was argument at lunch between the father and the son,
Smoke rose from Warsaw and the beef was underdone,
Nothing points to heaven now but the anti-aircraft gun:
>   With a hey nonny nonny
>   And a hi-de-ho.

Oh, the 'twenties and the 'thirties were not otherwise designed,
Than other times when blind men into ditches led the blind,
When the rich mouse ate the cheese and the poor mouse got the
>   rind,
And man, the self-destroyer, was not lucid in his mind:
>   With a hey nonny nonny
>   And a hi-de-ho.

WILLIAM PLOMER

To Any Member Of My Generation

What is it you remember? – the summer mornings
Down by the river at Richmond with a girl,
And as you kissed, clumsy in bathing costumes,
History guffawed in a rosebush. What a warning –
If only we had known, if only we had known!
And when you looked in mirrors was this meaning
Plain as the pain in the centre of a pearl?
Horrible tomorrow in Teutonic postures
Making absurd the past we cannot disown?

Whenever we kissed we cocked the future's rifles
And from our wild-oat words, like dragons' teeth,
Death underfoot now arises; when we were gay

Dancing together in what we hoped was life,
Who was it in our arms but the whores of death
Whom we have found in our beds today, today?

GEORGE BARKER

From *Autumn Journal*

Today was a beautiful day, the sky was a brilliant
  Blue for the first time for weeks and weeks
But posters flapping on the railings tell the fluttered
  World that Hitler speaks, that Hitler speaks
And we cannot take it in and we go to our daily
  Jobs to the dull refrain of the caption 'War'
Buzzing around us as from hidden insects
  And we think 'This must be wrong, it has happened before,
Just like this before, we must be dreaming;
  It was long ago these flies
Buzzed like this, so why are they still bombarding
  The ears if not the eyes?'
And we laugh it off and go round town in the evening
  And this, we say, is on me;
Something out of the usual, a Pimm's Number One, a Picon –
  But did you see
The latest? You mean whether Cobb has just bust the record
  Or do you mean the Australians have lost their last by ten
Wickets or do you mean that the autumn fashions –
  No, we don't mean anything like that again.
No, what we mean is Hodza, Henlein, Hitler,
  The Maginot Line,
The heavy panic that cramps the lungs and presses
  The collar down the spine.
And when we go out into Piccadilly Circus
  They are selling and buying the late

Special editions snatched and read abruptly
    Beneath the electric signs as crude as Fate.
And the individual, powerless, has to exert the
    Powers of will and choice
And choose between enormous evils, either
    Of which depends on somebody else's voice.
The cylinders are racing in the presses,
    The mines are laid,
The ribbon plumbs the fallen fathoms of Wall Street,
    And you and I are afraid.

LOUIS MACNEICE

From *September 1, 1939*

I sit in one of the dives
On Fifty-Second Street
Uncertain and afraid
As the clever hopes expire
Of a low dishonest decade:
Waves of anger and fear
Circulate over the bright
And darkened lands of the earth,
Obsessing our private lives;
The unmentionable odour of death
Offends the September night.

Accurate scholarship can
Unearth the whole offence
From Luther until now
That has driven a culture mad,
Find what occurred at Linz,
What huge imago made
A psychopathic god:

I and the public know
What all schoolchildren learn,
Those to whom evil is done
Do evil in return.

W. H. AUDEN

Autumn, 1939

The beech boles whiten in the swollen stream;
Their red leaves, shaken from the creaking boughs,
Float down the flooded meadow, half in dream,
Seen in a mirror cracked by broken vows.

Water-logged, slower, deeper, swirling down
Between the indifferent hills who also saw
Old jaundiced knights jog listlessly to town
To fight for love in some unreal war.

Black leaves are piled against the roaring weir;
Dark closes round the manor and the hut;
The dead knight moulders on his rotting bier,
And one by one the warped old casements shut.

ALUN LEWIS

Take Your Gun

Now As Then

When under Edward or Henry the English armies
Whose battles are brocade to us and stiff in tapestries
On a green and curling sea set out for France,
The Holy Ghost moved the sails, the lance
Was hung with glory, and in all sincerity
Poets cried 'God will grant to us the victory'.
For us, who by proxy inflicted gross oppression,
Among whom the humblest have some sins of omission,
War is not simple; in more or less degree
All are guilty, though some will suffer unjustly.
Can we say Mass to dedicate our bombs?
Yet those earlier English, for all their psalms,
Were marauders, had less provocation than we,
And the causes of war were as mixed and hard to see.
Yet since of two evils our victory would be the less,
And coming soon, leave some strength for peace,
Like Minot and the rest, groping we pray:
'Lord, turn us again, confer on us a victory.'

ANNE RIDLER

Man, Take Your Gun

Man, take your gun: and put to shame
earthquake and plague, the acts of God.
You maim the crazy and the lame.

Terror is their palsy, the knees
of men buckle for fear of man.
You are the God whom frenzy pleases.

You are the gas-man, and the flier
who drops his bomb; the man in tanks.
You wire mines and fear the fire.

And dig the hollow street with trenches
the gas-main and the sewer cross.
The stench of dead men makes you flinch.

But if the dying whimper, pain
pricks you like courage, like delight.
The vein sings to the cruel brain.

What are you, man, that gun in hand
with savagery and pity go,
and face to face with madness stand;

and acid-drenched and poison-sprayed
see flame run lovely like a wake
from raiders; and the burning lake
shake overhead? You are afraid.

The shadow flickers on the wall
like morse, like gun-shot. Terror walks
the tall roofs where the snipers hawk.
He stalks you, man. And, man, you fall.

J. BRONOWSKI

Thoughts On The Eve

I could love life the more
Would it but pass away
As quietly as the day
Ebbs from the darkening star

This dearly cherished thought,
Deep and enraptured pain,
Soothes like a gentle rain
My wild tempestuous heart.

To sail a billowing sea
And watch the departing shore
From a tall sea-girt tower
Is to die splendidly.

But to my chosen end
I would more humbly creep
As men weary for sleep
Pray darkness descend.

But should some savage Hand
My rising manhood stem,
Torn, haunted by its dream,
From Time, lonely to stand;

Life had I loved the more
Had it but passed away
As quietly as the day
Ebbs from the darkening star.

EMANUEL LITVINOFF

Two Pairs Of Shoes

Draw back the curtains,
Dim the electric light.
Now the stage is set for
Our impromptu first night.

We've had no rehearsals,
We don't need the cues,
And out in the corridor
Are two pairs of shoes.

If I could find the time, dear,
By looking in your eyes,
I'd never find the time for
God and apple pies.

If love was set to music,
And played at Albert Hall,
Man would love his neighbour,
There'd be no war at all.

Whisper, dear, you love me:
That's all you need to say.
Tomorrow I must leave my heart
For you to take away.

There's no time to lose, dear,
There's no time to lose.
Already they are polishing
Our two pairs of shoes.

KEITH FOOTTIT
killed in action, 1944

To Certain Ladies, On Going To The Wars

Goodbye ladies, O ladies sweet, goodbye,
No more the gentle flowers,
Another life I'll try.
No more the scented evenings,

The tussles in the hay,
It's time that I was leaving
To live another way.

O, there'll be blood, my ladies
(And not all mine, I hope),
And damp beds under hedges
And washing without soap.
Black lice will bite the body
That knew your friendly limbs;
In barrack-blocks I'll envy
Your silken-sheeted rooms.

But goodbye ladies, O ladies don't complain,
It's time I learnt to shoot straight
Or fly an aeroplane.
So many lads I knew once
Are rotting under sods:
I owe them this one journey –
So farewell, pretty birds.

HENRY TREECE

Recruiting Drive

Under the willow the willow
    I heard the butcher-bird sing,
Come out you fine young fellow
    From under your mother's wing.
I'll show you the magic garden
    That hangs in the beamy air,
The way of the lynx and the angry Sphinx
    And the fun of the freezing fair.

Lie down lie down with my daughter
   Beneath the Arabian tree,
Gaze on your face in the water
   Forget the scribbling sea.
Your pillow the nine bright shiners
   Your bed the spilling sand,
But the terrible toy of my lily-white-boy
   Is the gun in his innocent hand.

You must take off your clothes for the doctor
   And stand as straight as a pin,
His hand of stone on your white breast-bone
   Where the bullets all go in.
They'll dress you in lawn and linen
   And fill you with Plymouth gin,
O the devil may wear a rose in his hair
   I'll wear my fine doe-skin.

My mother weeps as I leave her
   But I tell her it won't be long,
The murderers wail in Wandsworth Gaol
   But I shoot a more popular song.
Down in the enemy country
   Under the enemy tree
There lies a lad whose heart has gone bad
   Waiting for me, for me.

He says I have no culture
   And that when I've stormed the pass
I shall fall on the farm with a smoking arm
   And ravish his bonny lass.
Under the willow the willow
   Death spreads her dripping wings
And caught in the snare of the bleeding air
   The butcher-bird sings, sings, sings.

CHARLES CAUSLEY

Epilogue

From the stern casement
　　Now shuttered and barred
Into the heavens
　　Moonless, unstarred,
When the last battle
　　Has broken the night,
Out of the darkness,
　　There shall come light.

Though the old beggar
　　Still plays his lute,
Crazily, lazily,
　　While we watch, mute,
The poet's sad song
　　Shall awaken the night
With its message of magic,
　　Until there is light.

PETER BAKER

The New Learning

Advice For A Journey

The drums mutter for war and soon we must begin
To seek the country where they say that joy
Springs flowerlike among the rocks, to win
The fabulous golden mountain of our peace.

O my friends, we are too young
For explorers, have no skill nor compass,
Nor even that iron certitude which swung
Our fathers at their self-fulfilling North.

So take no rations, remember not your homes –
Only the blind and stubborn hope to track
This wilderness. The thoughtful leave their bones
In windy foodless meadows of despair.

Never look back, nor too far forward search
For the white Everest of your desire;
The screes roll underfoot and you will never reach
Those brittle peaks which only clouds may walk.

Others have come before you. The immortal
Live like reflections and their frozen faces
Will give you courage to ignore the subtle
Sneer of the gentian and the iceworn pebble.

The fifes cry death and the sharp winds call.
Set your face to the rock; go on, go out
Into the bad lands of battle, into the cloud-wall
Of the future, my friends, and leave your fear.

Go forth, my friends, the raven is no sibyl;
Break the clouds' anger with your unchanged faces.
You'll find, maybe, the dream under the hill –
But never Canaan, nor any golden mountain.

SIDNEY KEYES

The New Learning

With hatred now all lips and wings
the human mind does silly things.
Common sense has fled, and reason
is definitely out of season.

In nature class the schoolboy's head
is taught to contemplate, instead
of flower pot and cactus stump,
a budding aluminium dump.

Can God that made the cactus grow
do miracles, he wants to know?
Can He that made the water wine
make Spitfires of a pot and pan?

He knows that, loving human life,
God strongly disapproves of strife
and doesn't care a damn for guns
except if they are British ones.

'The British blockade will bring salvation'
(he's told) 'to every neutral nation.
So starve them! then, their lands restored,
they'll all be free to praise the Lord.

'You think the Bible's right – it ain't
now that a murderer's a saint.
The new commandment's "Thou shalt kill
in order to effect God's will".'

And so with tanks for people's toes
the Christian soldier onward goes.

IAN SERRAILLIER

The Recruit

Pried from the circle where his family ends,
Man on his own, no hero of old tales,
Discovers when the pose of lone wolf fails
Loneliness and, miraculously, friends.

Finds how his comradeship with one depends
On being both from London, say, or Wales,
How with the next a common job prevails,
Sport with a third, and so the list extends.

Nation and region, class and craft and syndicate
Are only some: all attributes connect
Their owner with his kind, call him to vindicate

A common honour; and his self-respect
Starts from the moment when his senses indicate
'I' as a point where circles intersect.

JOHN MANIFOLD

Tell Us The Tricks

Say, soldier! Tell us the tricks,
    the tackle of your trade;
The passage of your hours;
    the plans that you have made –
Of what do you think – what consider?
Tell us of the slow process,
That gradual change
    from man to soldier – ?

And what can I say, what reply?
    There is no answer.
The tale is hidden in the eye.
The soldier's here – the man is not;
Man's voice was lost;
The sex decayed
By the bitter bayonet – the chattering shot
The growth delayed.
The brief days of youth,
And its forgotten past,
Cannot be commanded to appear,
We hope they may at last
    – some other time – some different year.

PAUL SCOTT

Squadding

The sergeant's roar, interpreted aright
by instinct of fear, dies bouncing on the asphalt.
The squad, grey-denimed in the distinct light
stand-easy, adjust a cap or finger a belt.

Shedding its shell, a crab must feel like this,
lost between two worlds, not so much scared as wary.
They consider the sergeant without prejudice
and accept the insulting candour of his stare.

Why is it then that with arms and legs loosened
out of a random rhythm they are forced to move
in a strange unison? Apart from the nuisance,
there is a buoyancy, even a kind of love.

Yet still, as the clue's emerging, they feel again
that pull of difference splitting each life into two.
More than the sergeant, each stands apart. The brain
is numbed with a semi-defiance. It isn't true.

It isn't true, each insists. It isn't happening.
This is not me. But it is. And you grin to find
the will re-welded, richer. You lose your cap,
feel foolish; and an urgency raps your mind –

tightened, look, in the buckle of belt and sling,
jestingly sealed in each momentous trifle,
stamped now, clamped in the bolt and the bayonet-ring,
fondled and final in the uplifted rifle.

JACK LINDSAY

Judging Distances

Not only how far away, but the way that you say it
Is very important. Perhaps you may never get
The knack of judging a distance, but at least you know
How to report on a landscape: the central sector,
The right of arc and that, which we had last Tuesday,
      And at least you know

That maps are of time, not place, so far as the army
Happens to be concerned – the reason being,
Is one which need not delay us. Again, you know
There are three kinds of tree, three only, the fir and the poplar,
And those which have bushy tops to; and lastly
    That things only seem to be things.

A barn is not called a barn, to put it more plainly,
Or a field in the distance, where sheep may be safely grazing.
You must never be over-sure. You must say, when reporting:
At five o'clock in the central sector is a dozen
Of what appear to be animals; whatever you do,
    Don't call the bleeders *sheep*.

I am sure that's quite clear; and suppose, for the sake of example,
The one at the end, asleep, endeavours to tell us
What he sees over there to the west, and how far away,
After first having come to attention. There to the west,
On the fields of summer and sun and the shadows bestow
    Vestments of purple and gold.

The still white dwellings are like a mirage in the heat,
And under the swaying elms a man and a woman
Lie gently together. Which is, perhaps, only to say
That there is a row of houses to the left of arc,
And that under some poplars a pair of what appear to be humans
    Appear to be loving.

Well that, for an answer, is what we might rightly call
Moderately satisfactory only, the reason being,
Is that two things have been omitted, and those are important.
The human beings, now: in what direction are they,
And how far away, would you say? And do not forget
    There may be dead ground in between.

There may be dead ground in between; and I may not have got
The knack of judging a distance; I will only venture
A guess that perhaps between me and the apparent lovers
(Who, incidentally, appear by now to have finished),
At seven o'clock from the houses, is roughly a distance
    Of about one year and a half.

HENRY REED

Naming Of Parts

Today we have naming of parts. Yesterday,
We had daily cleaning. And tomorrow morning,
We shall have what to do after firing. But today,
Today we have naming of parts. Japonica
Glistens like coral in all of the neighbouring gardens,
    And today we have naming of parts.

This is the lower sling swivel. And this
Is the upper sling swivel, whose use you will see,
When you are given your slings. And this is the piling swivel,
Which in your case you have not got. The branches
Hold in the gardens their silent, eloquent gestures,
    Which in our case we have not got.

This is the safety-catch, which is always released
With an easy flick of the thumb. And please do not let me
See anyone using his finger. You can do it quite easy
If you have any strength in your thumb. The blossoms
Are fragile and motionless, never letting anyone see
    Any of them using their finger.

And this you can see is the bolt. The purpose of this
Is to open the breech, as you see. We can slide it
Rapidly backwards and forwards: we call this

Easing the spring. And rapidly backwards and forwards
The early bees are assaulting and fumbling the flowers:
   They call it easing the Spring.

They call it easing the Spring: it is perfectly easy
If you have any strength in your thumb: like the bolt,
And the breech, and the cocking-piece, and the point of balance,
Which in our case we have not got; and the almond-blossom
Silent in all of the gardens and the bees going backwards and
                                 forwards,
   For today we have naming of parts.

HENRY REED

All Day It Has Rained

All day it has rained, and we on the edge of the moors
Have sprawled in our bell-tents, moody and dull as boors,
Groundsheets and blankets spread on the muddy ground
And from the first grey wakening we have found
No refuge from the skirmishing fine rain
And the wind that made the canvas heave and flap
And the taut wet guy-ropes ravel out and snap.
All day the rain has glided, wave and mist and dream,
Drenching the gorse and heather, a gossamer stream
Too light to stir the acorns that suddenly
Snatched from their cups by the wild south-westerly
Pattered against the tent and our upturned dreaming faces.
And we stretched out, unbuttoning our braces,
Smoking a Woodbine, darning dirty socks,
Reading the Sunday papers – I saw a fox
And mentioned it in the note I scribbled home; –
And we talked of girls and dropping bombs on Rome,
And thought of the quiet dead and the loud celebrities
Exhorting us to slaughter, and the herded refugees;

– Yet thought softly, morosely of them, and as indifferently
As of ourselves or those whom we
For years have loved, and will again
Tomorrow maybe love; but now it is the rain
Possesses us entirely, the twilight and the rain.

And I can remember nothing dearer or more to my heart
Than the children I watched in the woods on Saturday
Shaking down burning chestnuts for the schoolyard's merry play,
Or the shaggy patient dog who followed me
By Sheet and Steep and up the wooded scree
To the Shoulder o' Mutton where Edward Thomas brooded long
On death and beauty – till a bullet stopped his song.

                                        ALUN LEWIS

Winter Conscript

Who sees the moon over the hedgerows
like a pale scarecrow grinning,
sniffs from the lighted cookhouse shutter
the salt blue smoke of bacon frying;
who breaks his bread at the bare mess-table
asleep above his steaming porridge,
who cups his mug without a handle
sipping the watered beverage,
who from the bugle-call at dawn
until the evening's sad tattoo,
exists alone in memory,
finds snow reminds him of his lady.

Were not her limbs as pure as fallen star-shine;
her lips like berries gleaming in the cold?

Let him recall when separation grips him,
when emptiness and absence grow to pain,
the starveling image of so many singers
tortured by hunger, passion, prison, fame,
and most of all Villon – pick-purse Apollo –
crouched by some bake-house grating in the rain.

DEREK STANFORD

Instead Of A Carol

The winter hardens. Every night I hear
The patient khaki beast grieve in his stall,
His eyes behind the hard fingers soft as wool.
His cheerful morning face puts me in mind
Of certain things were remoured far and near
To hearts wherein there fretted and repined
A world that came to its last dated year.

RAYNER HEPPENSTALL
December 1940

Aldershot

Dark as if deep in Africa this town is lost
Away from the bright lights and the jokers
Persuading the hour to amuse. The quiet cafés
Where hearts are intruded among tea cups,
The stylish restaurant with waiters dancing like storks,
All these with the shadows at elegant bars
And the ladies in green at midnight parties
Join hands to escape this town, shun the roar
That is only echoing to the skies 'I forget, I forget'.
Soldiers have made here a drear country

Of barrack and ball-room, snack bar and square,
And the public-houses with their tired or joyful faces
Are signs of the disaster hitting us there.
Now all the world's darlings and mothers' heroes,
The lonely, the lovely, the shy and the bold,
Are made a machine or become hard hearted,
So fearful of memory that evenings lend
The power that preserves to a haunting end.

                                        JOHN WALLER

NAAFI Concert

Lulled by the painted voice, the shouting eyes
and the trembling legs of the little bleached soubrette
flashing their laughing, artificial lies,
the troops applaud whatever they can get.

Noble, she feels, her triumphed-mirrored hours,
amusing soldiers bored with baiting death —
'How grand they are', she thinks, 'these boys of ours!',
and shrieks more songs with harsh unsteady breath.

A quick swell rinses every emptied heart,
the lights go on all over the world again,
and she, a clever, saucy, passée tart
has won the wearing from their vacant strain.

The lights go on all over the world again,
the lights of yesterday's hopes and tomorrow's dreams
flicker across their boredom, fear and pain;
but love is further than in thought it seems.

So, as the clapped hands shape towards other aims,
the floor turned mirage and the dancer gone,
they drink their watery tea, play simple games
and think, the night is short, the day is long.

MAURICE LINDSAY

Army

Tomorrow and tomorrow and tonight,
Remorselessly the useless hours pass by
Without a pause: Old Time is sitting tight,
And men live here to learn to kill and die;
And day decays, slowly, meanly, falls
Into that well that living call the past
Like paper peeling from neglected walls.
Let us have some clean killing at the last!
We're tired of waste and muddle and the mind
Perpetually and helplessly confined
To barracks and parades upon a tidy square:
It's mad – the stupid and the humble folk
Are khaki heroes here, the beautiful's a swear
Word and our lives a dirty joke.

KENNETH NEAL

Soldier

I cannot know the man
Beneath this fighting skin;
The summer warns of death
For winter's underneath,
And in his straitened face,
The mouth and strap-firm chin,
Time shows his artifice,
Summer lets winter in.

Now he is dressed to kill,
But courts no summer girl
Deep in the mossy year,
To wait with lips and eyes
Wide in love's gravities,
His precious enterprise:
Time has clotted them all
In war's outrageous year.

Time gave a lying gift;
Arm is from arm bereft;
Married to his lath frame
Of bone, lean weapons claim
A ribbed affinity,
Barrel and shank agree,
By the same dream enmeshed,
And the one lust famished.

L. J. YATES

Heart's Song

Sing, Heart, a gay song,
Before my knees give way and I grovel;
Before I break from my own rein,
And the eyes of those that love me
See me a coward, and fill me with ice, despising!

Shut the door behind you tight,
There's no returning.
In memory your tears will flow
For home's peace yearning.
Pretend you have no mother,
No soft-eyed love,
Pretend you hate your brother

. . . O, Christ above . . .
Forget that hedgerows shelter lambs,
The clover stems are sweet,
Forget you plucked her cowslips
Where other lovers meet.

Sing, Heart! Quickly, sing loudly
Some song to take from me this fear;
Take hold of this blade, and drag it,
Drag it by chorus and joke, ruthlessly,
Before it kills me, from my naked heart.

Laugh and sing, laugh and sing,
Laugh and sing at anything,
Laugh till you close your eyes with mirth.
This your only rest on earth –
Learn to laugh until you're blind,
And then the Fear that lurks behind
Will not be seen, will not be known,
Until you meet, unarmed, alone.
He who stops laughing and opens his eyes
Meets Death ten times before he dies.

Give me a song, Heart, to sing loudly;
Something bold and without meaning,
Like a drum, like a drum, like a drum.
Sing quickly, Heart, in a strong voice
Before it is too late and my lips tremble,
A gay song, careless and free, powerful, blind,
Like a swinging, booted, marching-step,
Full of unthinking machine-courage,
Like a boot, shining and heavy, unfeeling, thick.

I looked at Heart, the hot tears through,
And saw that Heart was crying too.

RICHARD SPENDER
killed in action, 1943

When No Allies Are Left

The English War

Praise God, now, for an English war –
     The grey tide and the sullen coast,
The menace of the urgent hour,
The single island, like a tower,
     Ringed with an angry host.

This is the war that England knows,
     When all the world holds but one man –
King Philip of the galleons,
Louis, whose light outshone the sun's,
     The conquering Corsican;

When Europe, like a prison door,
     Clangs; and the swift, enfranchised sea
Runs narrower than a village brook;
And men who love us not, yet look
     To us for liberty;

When no allies are left, no help
     To count upon from alien hands,
No waverers remain to woo,
No more advice to listen to,
     And only England stands.

This is the war we always knew,
     When every county keeps her own,
When Kent stands sentry in the lane,
And Fenland guards her dyke and drain,
     Cornwall, her cliffs of stone;

When from the Cinque Ports and the Wight,
    From Plymouth Sound and Bristol Town,
There comes a noise that breaks our sleep,
Of the deep calling to the deep
    Where the ships go up and down,

And near and far across the world
    Hold open wide the water-gates,
And all the tall adventurers come
Homeward to England, and Drake's drum
    Is beaten through the Straits.

This is the war that we have known
    And fought in every hundred years,
Our sword, upon the last, steep path,
Forged by the hammer of our wrath
    On the anvil of our fears.

Send us, O God, the will and power
    To do as we have done before;
The men that ride the sea and air
Are the same men their fathers were
    To fight the English war.

And send, O God, the English peace –
    Some sense, some decency, perhaps
Some justice, too, if we are able,
With no sly jackals round our table,
    Cringing for blood-stained scraps;

No dangerous dreams of wishful men
    Whose homes are safe, who never feel
The flying death that swoops and stuns,
The kissing of the curtseying guns
    Slavering their streets with steel;

No dreams, Lord God, but vigilance,
    That we may keep, by might and main,
Inviolate seas, inviolate skies; —
But, if another tyrant rise,
    Then we shall fight again.

DOROTHY L. SAYERS

1940

From *Letters To Malaya*

How close to miracle seemed that retreat;
As if, by some providential cheat,
Victory had been defeated by defeat,
The winged eluded by the broken-winged!
Yet still our coasts with hazards huge were ringed,
Waiting to strike. For France was prostrate then,
And France's victor marshalling his men
To give his victory its final form.
Eerie the hush in England ere the storm:
Still skies, the stillness heralding disaster;
And one man's voice, the situation's master.
One man, whose very blemishes seemed great;
Whose life, had Rome not England been his state,
Plutarch had loved to write, and North translate;
Who time on time in those dumbfounding days
Rallied his country round a famous phrase,
Opposing to the other's frenzied fit
Calm eloquence and chuckle-stirring wit;
For not alone with Nazis was his feud,
Stern foe to Hitler — and to platitude.

MARTYN SKINNER

The Stand-To

Autumn met me today as I walked over Castle Hill.
The wind that had set our corn by the ears was blowing still:
Autumn, who takes the leaves and the long days, crisped the air
With a tang of action, a taste of death; and the wind blew fair

From the east for men and barges massed on the other side –
Men maddened by numbers or stolid by nature, they have their pride
As we in work and children, but now a contracting will
Crumples their meek petitions and holds them poised to kill.

Last night a Stand-To was ordered. Thirty men of us here
Came out to guard the star-lit village – my men who wear
Unwitting the season's beauty, the received truth of the spade –
Roadmen, farm labourers, masons, turned to another trade.

A dog barked over the fields, the candle stars put a sheen
On the rifles ready, the sandbags fronded with evergreen:
The dawn wind blew, the stars winked out on the posts where we lay,
The order came, Stand Down, and thirty went away.

Since a cold wind from Europe blows back the words in my teeth,
Since autumn shortens the days and the odds against our death,
And the harvest moon is waxing and high tides threaten harm,
Since last night may be the last night all thirty men go home.

I write this verse to record the men who have watched with me –
Spot who is good at darts, Squibby at repartee,
Mark and Cyril, the dead shots, Ralph with a ploughman's gait,
Gibson, Harris and Long, old hands for the barricade,

Whiller the lorry-driver, Francis and Rattlesnake,
Fred and Charl and Stan – these nights I have lain awake
And thought of my thirty men and the autumn wind that blows
The apples down too early and shatters the autumn rose.

Destiny, History, Duty, Fortitude, Honour – all
The words of the politicians seem too big or too small
For the ragtag fighters of lane and shadow, the love that has grown
Familiar as working-clothes, faithful as bone to bone.

Blow, autumn wind, upon orchard and rose! Blow leaves along
Our lanes, but sing through me for the lives that are worth a song!
Narrowing days have darkened the vistas that hurt my eyes,
But pinned to the heart of darkness a tattered fire-flag flies.

C. DAY LEWIS

Sentry Duty

His box is like a coffin, but erect,
the night is dull as death; he must not sleep,
but leans against the boards. The night winds creep
around his face, while the far stars reflect
the awful emptiness of heart and brain,
and trembling wires wail a requiem.
(If they were Sirens he would follow them
to the sweet morgue, their magical domain.)

But no one passes; a stray cat cries out,
the moon emerges from a cloud's dark rim,
and vanishes; he walks, and turns about.

Next day no sad unrest bewilders him
who'd seen the planets fall into a trance,
the earth shed lustre and significance.

MICHAEL HAMBURGER

Unseen Fire

This is a damned inhuman sort of war.
I have been fighting in a dressing-gown
Most of the night; I cannot see the guns,
The sweating gun-detachments or the planes;

I sweat down here before a symbol thrown
Upon a screen, sift facts, initiate
Swift calculations and swift orders; wait
For the precise split-second to order fire.

We chant our ritual words; beyond the phones
A ghost repeats the orders to the guns:
One Fire ... Two Fire ... ghosts answer: the guns roar
Abruptly; and an aircraft waging war
Inhumanly from nearly five miles height
Meets our bouquet of death -- and turns sharp right.

R. N. CURREY

State Of Readiness

The moon rises late:
After sudden warning we wait,
The guns manned, searching among the stars.
At last, perhaps, our hour has come. Cars
Shoot past with urgent messages. We stand
Eager and glad, rifles steady and cool in hand.
For months nothing has happened. Now the sky
Turns hostile. Around us searchlights pry

Into thin clouds. Tonight the enemy, unseen,
Is real. We know these tedious past days have been
Prelude to battle: and if the time is near,
No dearer thoughts shall resurrect our fear.
For this we have waited. If the air should fill
With mushroom parachutes we will
Forsake all memory, all promises to break
On future days, for battle's compelling sake.
We have been ready. Though the warning prove
As false as any, we have abjured our love,
All dreams or hopes, to keep alert and sure.
The drone of planes continues and clouds endure
The searchlight's naked steel. Flares fall,
Hang in the sky. Flashes of guns appal
The quiet air. But as the minutes pass
Talk dies out, rats scurry through the grass.
We grow tired, long for cigarettes. Our minds return
To windows where familiar lights still burn.
Our thoughts resume their island voyages:
Raiders give place to homelier images.
      The moon is full and shines
On tree and hill. In the farm a dog whines;
The routine of life continues while we wait;
Less eager and less certain. Our moons rise late.

H. B. MALLALIEU

A.A. Battery: 1940

Sentry on picket – and unaccustomed power!
The slave is now a despot for an hour.
Cerberus of these clanging bars
I search all faces: the uneasy cower
Out of my bayonet's gleam, while Mars

Gloats his approval from above the watch-tower.
Oh cynic pyramid of stars
To comfort *me*, yet promise *him* new wars.

By dawn the guard-room's fetid with the heat
Of dozing men: the dubbin and sweat of feet,
Seeping through leather, have begun
Inroads on sleep. The food we had hoped to eat
After our watching should be done
Is shrivelled. Men shudder, waking. In the street
A footstep rings towards the sun
Amen to this ordeal each night undergone.

Day grows; and now the air begins to beat
With many musics. Some, scarcely heard, are sweet,
Rung in the throats of birds: but one
Is crueller, harsh, insistent, music of sleet,
Symbol of hatred never done –
The enemy's dawn patrol. And that eagle fleet
That climbs the horizon with each sun
Draws the last, deepest music from our gun.

STEPHEN HAGGARD
died on active service, 1943

The Blazing Fire

Ballad Of The Safe Area

A little reading and a little loving
A little eating and a little sleeping
The days went over me half happy
With friends and books and cups of coffee

I watched the trees wave in green gardens
Avoided the police and the air raid wardens
I was delighted when the roses
Showed, like pups, their soft pink noses

Enjoyed the quiet and garrulous evenings
The rhythm of my child's deep breathing
As smoke and faces wove warm patterns
Of home not easily forgotten.

I thought of poets lost in barracks
Or crawling about on muddy stomachs
And drank their toasts in beer and whisky
Drank now to Stalin, now to Trotsky

Now to Chamberlain or Churchill
– In fact I wished nobody ill
But loved myself and forgave the devil
And tried, for a time, to live on the level

Lectured each morning to pale students
Taught them intriguing rudiments
Of revolution and laissez-faire
And above all, how to be debonair

So far, so good: the Spring was springing
Through purple heather to brown hills clinging
When over the city the planes came flying
And out I ran with the fear of dying

All night we stood out on the terrace
Watching the glow grow to a furnace
Bombs and shells and whirls of shrapnel
Laid us often on the gravel

Then in the middle of the bombardment
When the whole street was making friends
A landmine fell at the nearest corner
And I thought for a minute I was a gonner

Glass flowed like water from all the windows
Black smoke came rushing out in billows
A hundred doors leaped off their hinges
And I said goodbye to books and binges

Then a second landmine dropped just near
At the back of the house where lay my dear
But it didn't explode and I laughed and cried
And cursed as I pulled the family outside

Then along to the bridge where the flats were burning
I didn't look twice but improved my running
With the kid in my arms and the people crying
Past where the dead lay with the dying

But there was nothing for me to do
The wardens don't like you to be a hero
So they pushed me back from the blazing fire
And made me fall over some copper wire

Which made me feel rather a fool.
We all passed the night in a draughty school
And all caught colds, and that is why
Tears are still floating in my eye.

FRANCIS SCARFE

Night Raid

The sleepers humped down on the benches,
The daft boy was playing rummy with anyone he could get,
And the dancing girl said, 'What I say is,
If there's a bomb made for YOU,
You're going to get it.'
Someone muttered, 'The bees are coming again.'
Someone whispered beside me in the darkness,
'They're coming up from the east.'
Way off the guns muttered distantly.

This was in the small hours, at the ebb.
And the dancing girl clicked her teeth like castanets
And said, 'I don't mind life, believe me.
I like it. If there's any more to come,
I can take it and be glad of it.'
She was shivering and laughing and throwing her head back.
On the pavement men looked up thoughtfully,
Making plausible conjectures. The night sky
Throbbed under the cool bandage of the searchlights.

DESMOND HAWKINS

The Bomb Crater

The night struck lightning from the grass and split
The turfs of gentle lawns; it tore away
The fixed and certain oak, and carved a pit

Harsh as a dagger's knife in blood-red clay.
Nettles and nightshade dressed the wounded land
In wind-responsive folds, their roofs for balm;
And moveless water, with a cool green hand
Has soothed the rawness to reflective calm.
Resentful of these false cloaks of disguise,
And scrabbling at the crater's edge to climb
Back to the day, the limbless oak trunk lies –
Its roots left deep beyond the count of time,
Its body knotted in the flailing rage
Of gods uprooted for this rootless age.

JOHN ARLOTT

Bombs On My Town

The farmers I spoke of that night
In London, drive into High Street
A roundabout way,
Their stunted, aggressive features
More death-vacant than ever,
Since yesterday.

Quiet, an empty dray
Only to mark for this scooped-hollow
Yeomanry, its past proud chatter,
Its market clatter
Of carriage and horse,
Now a sad echo,
An exhumed decay.

The tradesmen I've known for years
Bow with civic ponderosity
Over smashed pavements, to collect

Their stock, swept, with their integrity,
Beneath the quick stroke
Of an uncaring raider,
Whose fifth-rate dentistry tore
Our houses from the long, gaping maw
Of High Street.

To see your small, damaged town
Where each stone
Holds a history of its own,
Evokes a wild pity
Deeper than being
With strange folk; seeing
The devastation
Of their city . . .

CHARLES HAMBLETT

Rural Raid

Earth opens where the squandered bombs fall wide
And all our view's a burning countryside.
Each fairy-lamp incendiary that falls
Is like a juggler adding to his balls
Tossing up more, to glitter every colour,
And when one's watched an hour, there's nothing duller.
Only the sudden metal weight of fear
Brings back the platitude that life is dear,
Keeps us awake while we sit staring out
With Reason pounding, 'What's it all about?'

DENTON WELCH

Air Raid Across The Bay At Plymouth

I

Above the whispering sea
And waiting rocks of black coast,
Across the bay, the searchlight beams
Swing and swing back across the sky.

Their ends fuse in a cone of light
Held for a bright instant up
Until they break away again
Smashing that image like a cup.

II

Delicate aluminium girders
Project phantom aerial masts
Swaying crane and derrick
Above the sea's just lifting deck.

III

Triangles, parallels, parallelograms,
Experiment with hypotheses
On the blackboard sky,
Seeking that X
Where the enemy is met.
Two beams cross
To chalk his cross.

IV

A sound, sounding ragged, unseen
Is chased by two swords of light.
A thud. An instant when the whole night gleams.
Gold sequins shake out of a black-silk screen.

V

Jacob ladders slant
Up to the god of war
Who, from his heaven-high car,
Unloads upon a star
A destroying star.

Round the coast, the waves
Chuckle between rocks.
In the fields the corn
Sways, with metallic clicks.
Man hammers nails in Man,
High on his crucifix.

STEPHEN SPENDER

Written From Plymouth

Written from Plymouth where portentous mist
Passes its hands across the tattered theatres'
Faces, hit houses hate to hate but must;

Recumbent Sunderlands all afternoon
As well-fed manatees wait on the water
And a destroyer sprints from swoon to swoon;

The hawsers of balloons above the Hoe
Lead to a kind of unkind smile, Drake's Island
Scowls through its barrack windows at the slow

Horizon wriggle; while those high hotels
The 'Lockyer' 'Continental' 'Duke of Cornwall'
Lick their cracked lips of steps, for pleasure sells

Providing pain provides it gladly. Most
Like unpretending children Plymouth quivers,
Its thoughts apparent in each cast and mast.

DRUMMOND ALLISON
killed in action, 1943

A Refusal To Mourn The Death, By Fire, Of A Child In London

Never until the mankind making
Bird beast and flower
Fathering and all humbling darkness
Tells with silence the last light breaking
And the still hour
Is come of the sea tumbling in harness

And I must enter again the round
Zion of the water bead
And the synagogue of the ear of corn
Shall I let pray the shadow of a sound
Or sow my salt seed
In the least valley of sackcloth to mourn

The majesty and burning of the child's death.
I shall not murder
The mankind of her going with a grave truth
Nor blaspheme down the stations of the breath
With any further
Elegy of innocence and youth.

Deep with the first dead lies London's daughter,
Robed in the long friends,
The grains beyond age, the dark veins of her mother,

Secret by the unmourning water
Of the riding Thames.
After the first death, there is no other.

DYLAN THOMAS

Elegy On A City

The city, forty miles away,
Once had a heart but made of stone.
The face we classified as stone
Haunted like flesh and fell apart.

Watching from this secluded bay
We see the flame and in our loss
Can realise the greater loss,
The human misery and shame.

But this is abstract like a play
In which the scenic properties
Move and are more than properties,
The grass is greener than real green.

Such never was the human way,
We live in pain but do not grieve.
The city burns, we do not grieve.
Grief can live only in the brain.

The city burns, alas, we say,
But human hope is never dead.
The bone may crack to reach the dead
But still the foolish spirits grope

And murmur, 'We're alive today.
The city burns but still we love.
All that we know is pain and love.
And once again the spring returns.'

And once again the spring returns.

                                        JULIAN SYMONS

Ragnarok

Our Trojan world is polarised to mourn;
To dream and find a black spot on the sun,
And wake to love and find the lover gone.

The destination of any weapon is grief.
In homesteads now where joy must seem naive
Under a splitting sky our women conceive.

The towns of houses, massed security
Out-generalled by a later century,
Are hearse-plumes on an old economy.

The ache of crushed walls when the raid is over.
This is a house, we said, we have built forever:
A two-backed fool, thinking of one day's weather.

Only one monster has to love his error.
Only his wrangling heart cannot recover,
But glories in illusion when half cadaver;

Or likes being ill, or nurses grievances,
Or calls a mountain or a forest 'his',
Or quarrels in five hundred languages.

And man, erect, unvenerable,
A bloodshot eye so simply vulnerable
That half his history is marginal,

Incises stone in the Bastille of hate:
'Give us this day before it is too late
Something to love indeed, enough to eat.'

KENNETH ALLOTT

These Are Facts

These are facts, observe them how you will:
Forget for a moment the medals and the glory,
The clean shape of the bomb, designed to kill,
And the proud headlines of the papers' story.

Remember the walls of brick that forty years
Had nursed to make a neat though shabby home;
The impertinence of death, ignoring tears,
That smashed the house and left untouched the Dome.

Bodies in death are not magnificent or stately,
Bones are not elegant that blast has shattered;
This sorry, stained and crumpled rag was lately
A man whose life was made of little things that mattered;

Now he is just a nuisance, liable to stink,
A breeding-ground for flies, a test-tube for disease:
Bury him quickly and never pause to think,
What is the future worth to men like these?

People are more than places, more than pride;
A million photographs record the works of Wren;
A city remains a city on credit from the tide
That flows among its rocks, a sea of men.

RUTHVEN TODD

Johnny The Bright Star

Airman

This is his path to the wind
the last white segment of the earth
he sprung from: and his birth
has come to this small cockpit
and this last white road
the earth has sinned.

This is his way to the sun
the airscrew turns and coughs,
breaks into thunder, he takes off
into the sunlit distances of space
and in one home
tears have begun.

This is his road to death
his last objective, and his coronation
the chosen king of a chosen nation
that has no land but love,
his posthumous decoration,
the sanction of his breath.

BRUCE BAIN

NAAFI At The Drome

Flushed faces of the young
like miniatures hung
upon grey walls of silence,
the smoke of myriad cigarettes
weaves through the hushed regrets
and lulls the violence.

The piano tinkles out its trite
reminders of their night
of dreams, with muffled glee
they sip their cup of bitter tea
at tables that are stained
as finally as their lives.

When they have gone, the room
retains its temperature of doom,
the smell of waste;
of stubbed out fags, stale tea
and that sharp memory
of the flushed faces of the young
hung, for ever, hung.

BRUCE BAIN

What I Never Saw

I was ready for death,
Ready to give my all in one expansive gesture
For a cause that was worthy of death.
I wanted to fear, to watch blood and torture,
To draw my last breath
Amidst a chaos of dramatic thunder.
I dreamt of aeroplanes sweeping the sky,
Gave war her ghastly lure,
Came, ready to fight and to die.

I thought in my mufti
Of brave men marching to battle
And came here to join them,
To share their machine guns' rattle.

What I never saw
Were the weary hours of waiting while the
                              sun rose and set,
The everlasting eye turned upwards to the sky
Watching the weather which said,
'Thou shalt not fly.'

We sat together as we sat at peace
Bound by no ideal of service
But by a common interest in pornography and
                              a desire to outdrink one another.
War was remote:
There was a little trouble in Abyssinia;
Some of us came from Kenya and said
'Why I was on the spot all the while
And the Italians sprayed the roadsides with
                              mustard gas.'
Theirs were the stories of war.

Then came the queueing, the recurrent line of
                              pungent men
Dressed in dirt with mud eating their trouser legs,
The collar that is cleaner than the shirt
And the inevitable adjectives.

The papers ran out early today,
There was no butter for the bread at breakfast,
Nobody calls us at dawn,
We never strain or sweat,
Nor do they notice when we come in late.

When I was a civilian I hoped high,
Dreamt my future cartwheels in the sky,
Almost forgot to arm myself

Against the boredom and the inefficiency
The petty injustice and the everlasting grudges.
The sacrifice is greater than I ever expected.

TIMOTHY CORSELLIS
killed in action, 1941

There Is A Meeting Place In Heaven

There is a meeting place in Heaven,
I have an appointment there with God;
I must come proudly to his palace
And beat his gates with a golden rod,

Enter and say 'Through life I passed
With little honour and with great conceit:
In life I was most unworthy
Of eyes that saw and a heart that beat,

But in death, but in death
I acted my part in an heroic
Which has taken away the firmament's breath.'.

TIMOTHY CORSELLIS

War

When the bloom is off the garden,
and I'm fighting in the sky,
when the lawns and flower beds harden,
and when weak birds starve and die,
and death-roll will grow longer,

eyes will be moist and red;
and the more I kill, the longer
shall I miss friends who are dead.

NIGEL WEIR
killed in action, 1940

'Operations Calling!'

'*Clearing Black Section*
Patrol Bass Rock,'
Leaps heart; after shock
Action comes stumbling;
Snatch your helmet;
Then run smoothly, to the grumbling
Of a dozing Merlin heating
Supercharged air,
You are there
By 'Z'.

Down hard on the behind
The parachute; you are blind
With your oxygen snout
But click, click, click, click, you feel
And the harness is fixed.
Round the wing
And 'Out of the cockpit, you,'
Clamber the rung
And the wing as if a wasp had stung
You, hop and jump into the cockpit,
Split second to spike
The Sutton harness holes,
One, two, three, four,

Thrust with your
Hand to the throttle open ...

'*Operations*' called and spoken.

DAVID BOURNE
killed in action, 1941

It Is Death Now We Look Upon

Dayfall,
swallowsong,
murmurous the river
which is memory –

it is death now we look upon.

Now
hands have no meaning
eyes no longer speak
kisses call
sorrow, like a dream
out of the dusk
remembering

it is death now we look upon.

Wherefore
call home the old,
and let them lie
lapped in their shaken
yet unshaken, faith;

call home tomorrow's quick
the beautiful, the glad,
the unrelenting.
Call home the children
we have made,
but shall not know.

Cancel all tears,
and let all love
grow cold,
that pain may ease,
remembering

it is death now we look upon.

T. R. HODGSON
killed in action, 1941

Aircrew

The grasshopper Wellington comes in to land.
The hand on the levers is not my hand.
Mine are more stuck to earth and sand.

Permission to land on the rising ground.
Bandaged the casual aerial wound.
The pub on the hill has change for a pound.

Lying at last on the hugging bed.
The vertical toes and the parallel head.
There was something the girl in the photo said.

Born for a war or born for a game.
The factories are burning, but no one's to blame.
In a thousand years they'll be burning the same.

In the morning they land in the black ages field.
Sun in our air, touch down, and are concealed.
On an old earth: their sickness will be healed.

BRIAN ALLWOOD
killed in action, 1944

Pilot

The airman has nothing to say about this.
The moon is rising and she is not his,
Or wings are caking with malignant ice.

Distant the point where different language speaks.
The hours are minutes and the years are weeks.
The slow gulls wander; and the tracer streaks.

Has nothing to say, and this is done.
At night the long youth of the flaring gun;
Against the great raiders, the great sun.

Returning now the dawn lets him be safe:
No one has really asked him for his life,
Eating eggs and bacon with a fork and knife.

BRIAN ALLWOOD

Combat Report

Just then I saw the bloody Hun.
You saw the Hun? You, light and easy,
Carving the soundless daylight. *I was breezy
When I saw that Hun.* Oh wonder
Pattern of stress, of nerve poise, flyer,

Overtaking time. *He came out under*
Nine-tenths cloud, but I was higher.
Did Michelangelo aspire,
Painting the laughing cumulus, to ride
The majesty of air. *He was a trier*
I'll give him that, the Hun. So you convert
Ultimate sky to air speed, drift, and cover:
Sure with the tricky tools of God and lover.
I let him have a sharp four-second squirt,
Closing to fifty yards. He went on fire.
Your deadly petals painted, you exert
A simple stature. Man-high, without pride,
You pick your way through heaven and the dirt.
He burnt out in the air: that's how the poor sod died.

JOHN PUDNEY

For Johnny

Do not despair
For Johnny-head-in-air;
He sleeps as sound
As Johnny underground.

Fetch out no shroud
For Johnny-in-the-cloud;
And keep your tears
For him in after years.

Better by far
For Johnny-the-bright-star,
To keep your head,
And see his children fed.

JOHN PUDNEY

Missing

Less said the better.
The bill unpaid, the dead letter.
No roses at the end
Of Smith, my friend.

Last words don't matter,
And there are none to flatter.
Words will not fill the post
Of Smith, the ghost.

For Smith, our brother,
Only son of loving mother,
The ocean lifted, stirred,
Leaving no word.

JOHN PUDNEY

Reported Missing

With broken wing they limped across the sky
caught in late sunlight, with their gunner dead,
one engine gone, – the type was out-of-date, –
blood on the fuselage turning brown from red:

knew it was finished, looking at the sea
which shone back patterns in kaleidoscope
knew that their shadow would meet them by the way,
close and catch at them, drown their single hope:

sat in this tattered scarecrow of the sky
hearing it cough, the great plane catching
now the first dark clouds upon her wing-base, –
patching the great tear in evening mockery.

So two men waited, saw the third dead face,
and wondered when the wind would let them die.

JOHN BAYLISS

Poem

The pale wild roses star the banks of green
and poignant poppies startle their fields with red,
while peace like sunlight rests on the summer scene,
though lilac that flashed in hedges is dulled and dead:
in the faint sky the singing birds go over,
the sheep are quiet where the quiet grasses are.
I go to the plane among the peaceful clover,
but climbing in the Hampden, shut myself in war.

HERBERT CORBY

Missing

They told me, when they cut the ready wheat
the hares are suddenly homeless and afraid,
and aimlessly run the stubble with scared feet
finding no homes in sunlight or in shade.
– It's morning, and the Hampdens have returned,
the crews are home, have stretched and laughed and gone:
whence the planes came and the bright neon burned
the sun has ridden the sky and made the dawn.
He walks distraught, circling the landing ground,

waiting the last one in that won't come back,
and like those hares, he wanders round and round,
lost and desolate on the close-cropped track.

HERBERT CORBY

The Lost

Think of them. You did not die as these
   caged in an aircraft that did not return.
Whenever hearts have song and minds have peace
or in your eyes the prides of banners burn,
think of these who dreamed and loved as you,
   and gave their laughter, gave their sun and snow,
their English grave blessed by their native dew
   that you would live. To them this debt you owe.
Their glory shines about the sky for ever,
   though in these things they left to you, the ghost
should haunt your field of ease and resting river.
   Their lives are ended, but dreams are not yet lost
if you remember in your laugh and song
   these boys who do not sing and laughed not long.

HERBERT CORBY

One More Day of War

A Wartime Dawn

Dulled by the slow glare of the yellow bulb;
As far from sleep still as at any hour
Since distant midnight; with a hollow skull
In which white vapours seem to reel
Among limp muddles of old thought; till eyes
Collapse into themselves like clams in mud . . .
Hand paws the wall to reach the chilly switch;
Then nerve-shot darkness gradually shakes
Throughout the room. *Lie still* . . . Limbs twitch;
Relapse to immobility's faint ache. And time
A while relaxes; space turns wholly black.

But deep in the velvet crater of the ear
A chip of sound abruptly irritates.
A second, a third chirp; and then another far
Emphatic trill and chirrup shrills in answer; notes
From all directions round pluck at the strings
Of hearing with frail finely-sharpened claws.
And in an instant, every wakened bird
Across surrounding miles of air
Outside, is sowing like a scintillating sand
Its throat's incessantly replenished store
Of tuneless singsong, timeless, aimless, blind.

Draw now with prickling hand the curtains back;
Unpin the blackout-cloth; let in
Grim crack-of-dawn's first glimmer through the glass.
All's yet half sunk in Yesterday's stale death,
Obscurely still beneath a moist-tinged blank
Sky like the inside of a deaf mute's mouth . . .
Nearest within the window's sight, ash-pale

Against a cinder-coloured wall, the white
Pear-blossom hovers like a stare; rain-wet
The further housetops weakly shine; and there,
Beyond, hangs flaccidly a lone barrage-balloon.

An incommunicable desolation weighs
Like depths of stagnant water on this break of day. –
Long meditation without thought. – Until a breeze
From some pure Nowhere straying, stirs
A pang of poignant odour from the earth, an unheard sigh
Pregnant with sap's sweet tang and raw soil's fine
Aroma, smell of stone, and acrid breath
Of gravel puddles. While the brooding green
Of nearby gardens' grass and trees, and quiet flat
Blue leaves, the distant lilac mirages, are made
Clear by increasing daylight, and intensified.

Now head sinks into pillows in retreat
Before this morning's hovering advance;
(Behind loose lids, in sleep's warm porch, half hears
White hollow clink of bottles, – and dragging crunch
Of milk-cart wheels, – and presently a snatch
Of windy whistling as the newsboy's bike winds near,
Distributing to neighbour's peaceful steps
Reports of last-night's battles); at last sleeps.
While early guns on Norway's bitter coast
Where faceless troops are landing, renew fire:
And one more day of War starts everywhere.

DAVID GASCOYNE

At The Range

Through windows, as we marched, the distant rooms
Led us a moment back along the road. We saw again
The bureau open, the coloured vase of ferns,

Lilies' unvenomed fangs whose wound could yet cause pain.
Thatched houses stared indifferent to our claim:
And the church clock to stress our trespass there
Kept its own hour eternally at ten. A sudden climb
Turned from the village. Ahead the downs were bare.

Bullets speed towards a future day:
Each rifle cracks our whispering of the past.
The target changes as we fire: men who will die
Fall on the splintered chalk: until the eye sees at last
Only the dull butts and the warning red flag wave.
The acrid powder smells on our fingers. In groups we stand
Tall in this quarry where sun and shadow weave
Patterns of isolation, gulls over desolate sand.

Our minds from scattered journeys, concentrate
Upon the target rings. 'Inner at nine o'clock':
We are not thinking of an enemy, nor trite
Slogans of hate. We wait, loose-limbed, for shock.
The butt is firm, at home against the shoulder.
The bull obscures village and room from sight.
There is only this minute: each wholly a soldier.
I sense the birds above me flying into light.

After cigarettes we collect the flags,
Fold over groundsheets, march back to the 'drome.
Rain driven by April gusts stings against the face.
The village no longer offers an idea of home.
We quicken steps, eager to reach our huts;
Content at first to smoke or talk, as the wind
With envied fury beats against the walls:
Till thoughts of other rooms come back to mind.

H. B. MALLALIEU

A Journey Through A War

Silently Man across this valley
Moved through the thin rain's steel and thunder's volley,
    A figure through the pages of a fable,
    Obscure the moral and the fancy feeble.
      Later the land he entered, bending
Like branch before the winds, hardened to binding
    Frost and a winter more than nine days' wonder;
    Day dark as night, night certain death to wander.
      By snow concealed the tracks deceived him:
Skirting all dangers, his good star saved him,
    Led him at last, almost his last breath panting,
    To country, white, soft, smooth as oil-painting;
      Christmas world, but no birds, no people
      To celebrate the season. Willing pupil,
    He learned to bear the climate, was not wasteful
    Of Silence, though lonely at times and wistful
      For a well-loved land left at morning
Before the storm-clouds draped the skies in mourning
    And on his travels told a world was over
    And no redress and no returning ever.

GORDON SWAINE

Poem

I do not fear so much
The bitter, driving weather
Or loneliness in an iron hutch
In this dead expanse of heather

As I fear the possible day
Of stillness, when the process
Of war will lamely digress
To action's zero point, and stay.

I fear the vacant, future afternoon
When trumpet echoes or the creak of wheels,
Putting an edge upon the shallow tune
Out of the gramophone, will slyly steal

Up from the dead ground underneath the slopes
Of the placated memory and bite
In on the never, strike light
Upon the private guilt we'll dope

With level knowledge or the kick
Of atomising wit-fear the outcast seed
Whose conscious and malignant flowers will lick
Me with gross, petalled tongues that break and bleed

Over me all the blood I did not pity
Enough when I was told that it was shed
In Egypt or in Gaul or in some city
Razed by explosion, or thinned on the sea's bed.

I fear how lucidly I shall remember
That I dared contemplate a moment of time,
Without compassion, when men rushed to dismember
Mutually their white harmonious limbs –

And if, in the winter garden, again begins
That idle talk with cigarettes and tea,
I fear I shall need fear forgiveness for these sins
And make repentance my excuse to be.

W. F. M. STEWART

War Generation

We have hardly started to suck the core of the apple,
our gobbet of life is stranger still to the tongue;
we have scarcely yet forsaken the drying nipple
    for a man's place in the sun.

Only last week we laughed at the glimpse of a rainbow,
our toys of Monday are scarcely back on their tray;
we had never even learnt to see a Picasso,
    never, till yesterday.

Only this morning the telescope eye of the housefly
was ours to measure the constant path of the sun.
This morning the power and the madness to be, to *be*;
    yet tonight it is done.

For tonight we, old in our own generation,
have learnt the wisdom of segregating our days,
living each hour on the crumbs of a bargain broken,
    ignoring the haemorrhage.

But we cannot keep cheating for ever, we cannot pass
for ever the subtle sting of the codicil.
The vision devolves on others, so fetch the glass
    that *our* spring must fill.

                                        ALAN ROOK

Soldier's Song

O Death, be kind to the swaddie,
    The man with a load of bull –
Be kind to the muscled body
    Thumbs up and belly-full.

Browned-off with the bints and boozing,
   Sweating on news from home,
Bomb-happy, and scared of losing
   This tent of flesh and bone –

These prized, unique possessions;
   Quick hand and practised eye,
The senses at action-stations,
   Alert to perceive or die;

Gun-proud and proud of body,
   With stripped and easy mind:
O Death be kind to the swaddie,
   In whom our world shall find

Its seed and fierce begetting:
   The future and shining land
Sprung from our dark sun's setting –
   A harvest, bird in hand.

JOCELYN BROOKE

They Said That Life

They said that life was more than this,
   They said that other gods were good.
They whispered darkly of a bliss
   We did not know – and yet we could.

These were strange words. And we, afraid,
   Clung to our faith, the things we knew;
And to the one Lord God we prayed,
   And wondered if the words were true.

DAVID RAIKES
killed in action, 1945

Local Leave

In three or four or five weeks' time when I
Am out in Tripoli or Libya,
Or somewhere on the way to India,
I shall be listening quite convincedly

To lists of what we'd do if only we
Were back in England – where we'd go to eat,
And what we'd go to see, and how complete
A perfect day beneath a kinder sky.

Ironic, for tonight was my free night.
I'd waited for it all the week. I spent
An hour waiting for the bus. I went
Around closed shops in heavy, sleety rain,
Queued uselessly for flicks, came back again
To spend my Saturday evening on the site.

R. N. CURREY

Steel Cathedrals

It seems to me, I spend my life in stations.
Going, coming, standing, waiting.
Paddington, Darlington, Shrewsbury, York.
I know them all most bitterly.
Dawn stations, with a steel light, and waxen figures.
Dust, stone, and clanking sounds, hiss of weary steam.
Night stations, shaded light, fading pools of colour.
Shadows and the shuffling of a million feet.

Khaki, blue, and bulky kitbags, rifles gleaming dull.
Metal sound of army boots, and smoker's coughs.
Titter of harlots in their silver foxes.
Cases, casks, and coffins, clanging of the trolleys.
Tea urns tarnished, and the greasy white of cups.
Dry buns, Woodbines, Picture Post and Penguins;
and the blaze of magazines.
Grinding sound of trains, and rattle of the platform gates.
Running feet and sudden shouts, clink of glasses from the buffet.
Smell of drains, tar, fish and chips and sweaty scent, honk of taxis;
and the gleam of cigarettes.
Iron pillars, cupolas of glass, girders messed by pigeons;
the lazy singing of a drunk.
Sailors going to Chatham, soldiers going to Crewe.
Aching bulk of kit and packs, tin hats swinging.
The station clock with staggering hands and callous face,
says twenty-five-to-nine.
A cigarette, a cup of tea, a bun,
and my train goes at ten.

D. VAN DEN BOGAERDE

1943

Embarkation Song

Behind are the guns drilled by their daughters
Hills ahead like fumes in a retort,
Salt water beside me, an endless bay of water
Is there a way out?

A girl I know would hide me; she's no angel,
With a tribe's blood on her nails and lips.
We'd love and drown the war and then be single
At the war's end perhaps.

Or ask the chemist, delving in the daylight
Of shelves crowded with bitter looks.
Here's peace for sixpence; I can have myrrh and aconite
If I write in the book.

I'm joking, dear; and I shan't ask what you're doing
While I'm abroad, or how you wait.
But quick, tell me once more why I am going,
Before it is too late.

GEOFFREY MATTHEWS

The Desert

Egypt

Who knows the lights at last, who knows the cities
And the unloving hands upon the thighs
Would yet return to seek his home-town pretties
For the shy finger-tips and sidelong eyes.

Who knows the world, the flesh, the compromises
Would go back to the theory in the book:
Who knows the place the poster advertises
Back to the poster for another look.

But nets the fellah spreads beside the river
Where the green waters criss-cross in the sun
End certain migratory hopes for ever;
In that white light, all shadows are undone.

The desert slays. But safe from Allah's justice
Where the broad river of His Mercy lies,
Where ground for labour, or where scope for lust is,
The crooked and tall and cunning cities rise.

The green Nile irrigates a barren region,
All the coarse palms are ankle-deep in sand;
No love roots deep, though easy loves are legion:
The heart's as hot and hungry as the hand.

In airless evenings, at the café table,
The soldier sips his thick sweet coffee up:
The dry grounds, like the moral to my fable,
Are bitter at the bottom of the cup.

G. S. FRASER

Soldiers Bathing

The sea at evening moves across the sand.
Under a reddening sky I watch the freedom of a band
Of soldiers who belong to me. Stripped bare
For bathing in the sea, they shout and run in the warm air;
Their flesh worn by the trade of war, revives
And my mind towards the meaning of it strives.

All's pathos now. The body that was gross,
Rank, ravenous, disgusting in the act or in repose,
All fever, filth and sweat, its bestial strength
And bestial decay, by pain and labour grows at length
Fragile and luminous. 'Poor bare forked animal',
Conscious of his desires and needs and flesh that rise and fall,
Stands in the soft air, tasting after toil
The sweetness of his nakedness: letting the sea-waves coil
Their frothy tongues about his feet, forgets
His hatred of the war, its terrible pressure that begets
A machinery of death and slavery,
Each being a slave and making slaves of others: finds that he
Remembers his old freedom in a game
Mocking himself, and comically mimics fear and shame.

He plays with death and animality;
And reading in the shadows of his pallid flesh, I see
The idea of Michelangelo's cartoon
Of soldiers bathing, breaking off before they were half done
At some sortie of the enemy, an episode
Of the Pisan wars with Florence. I remember how he showed
Their muscular limbs that clamber from the water
And heads that turn across the shoulder, eager for the slaughter,
Forgetful of their bodies that are bare,

And hot to buckle on and use the weapons lying there.
– And I think too of the theme another found
When, shadowing men's bodies on a sinister red ground,
Another Florentine, Pollaiuolo –
Painted a naked battle: warriors, straddled, hacked the foe,
Dug their bare toes into the soil and slew
The brother-naked man who lay between their feet and drew
His lips back from his teeth in a grimace.

They were Italians who knew war's sorrow and disgrace
And showed the thing suspended, stripped: a theme
Born out of the experience of war's horrible extreme
Beneath a sky where even the air flows
With *lacrimae Christi*. For that rage, that bitterness, those blows,
That hatred of the slain, what could they be
But indirectly or directly a commentary
On the Crucifixion? And the picture burns
With indignation and pity and despair by turns
Because it is the obverse of the scene
Where Christ hangs murdered, stripped, upon the Cross. I mean,
That is the explanation of its rage.

And we too have out bitterness and pity that engage
Blood, spirit in this war. But night begins,
Night of the mind: who nowadays is conscious of our sins?
Though every human deed concerns our blood,
And even we must know, what nobody has understood,
That some great love is over all we do,
And that is what has driven us to this fury, for so few
Can suffer all the terror of that love:
The terror of that love has set us spinning in this groove
Greased with our blood.

       These dry themselves and dress,
Combing their hair, forget the fear and shame of nakedness.

Because to love is frightening we prefer
The freedom of our crimes. Yet, as I drink the dusky air,
I feel a strange delight that fills me full,
Strange gratitude, as if evil itself were beautiful,
And kiss the wound in thought, while in the west
I watch a streak of red that might have issued from Christ's breast.

F. T. PRINCE

Lecturing To Troops

They sit like shrubs among the cans and desert thistles
    in the tree's broken shade and the sea-glare:
strange violent men, with dirty unfamiliar muscles,
sweating down the brown breast, wanting girls and beer.
The branches shake down sand along a crawling air,
    and drinks are miles towards the sun
    and Molly and Polly and Pam are gone.

Waiting for my announcement, I feel neat and shy,
    foreign before their curious helplessness,
innocence bought by action, like the sea's amnesty:
all my clean cleverness is tiny, is a loss;
and it is useless to be friendly and precise
    – thin as a hornet in a dome
    against the cries of death and home.

How can they be so tolerant – they who have lost
    the kiss of tolerance – and patient to endure
calm unnecessity? They have walked horror's coast,
loosened the flesh in flame, slept with naked war:
while I come taut and scathless with a virgin air,
    diffident as a looking-glass,
    with the fat lexicon of peace.

The strangeness holds them: a new planet's uniform,
    grasped like the frilly pin-ups in their tent
– something without the urgency of hate and harm,
something forgotten.
            But that is not what I meant:
I should have been the miles that made them innocent,
    and something natural as the sun
    from the beginning to everyone
    though Harry and Larry and Len are gone.

TERENCE TILLER
Coastal Battery, Tripolitania, 1943

From *Eighth Army*

We ploughed the sand with shell and burning bomb
And found few bones there where we left our own
Bleached by the drifting detritus of stone,
Bright in their busy many-fingered tomb.

Myriads of little hands there were to clutch
And hold us, when we lay down to our rest,
Quiet of the torn and sun-enkindled breast,
Hands that were feverish and dry to touch.

The papers called us heroes, but we knew
A hero is a visionary being,
Uncomfortable to live with probably, –
In Greece perhaps you might find one or two.

We never liked them, and we hated sand
So loving warm, so thirsty for our blood;
But still they might have sent us into mud
A fathom deep – this was at least dry land.

But cold at night, a whisperer to the moon,
Where many of us with the dust of Kings
For coverlet rest from our wanderings,
Where even heroes are forgotten soon.

T. W. RAMSEY

El Alamein

There are flowers now, they say, at Alamein;
Yes, flowers in the minefields now.
So those that come to view that vacant scene
Where death remains and agony has been
Will find the lilies grow –
Flowers, and nothing that we know.

So they rang the bells for us and Alamein,
Bells which we could not hear:
And to those who heard the bells what could it mean,
That name of loss and pride, El Alamein?
– Not the murk and harm of war,
But their hope, their own warm prayer.

It will become a staid historic name,
That crazy sea of sand!
Like Troy or Agincourt its single fame
Will be the garland for our brow, our claim,
On us a fleck of glory to the end:
And there our dead will keep their holy ground.

But this is not the place that we recall,
The crowded desert crossed with foaming tracks,
The one blotched building, lacking half a wall,
The grey-faced men, sand powdered over all;
The tanks, the guns, the trucks,
The black, dark-smoking wrecks.

So be it: none but us has known that land:
El Alamein will still be only ours
And those ten days of chaos in the sand.
Others will come who cannot understand,
Will halt beside the rusty minefield wires
And find there – flowers.

JOHN JARMAIN
killed in action, 1944

From *Portrait And Background*

Tobruk way were the graves. Not many,
As numbers go, as casualties in war,
Though in the isolating moon they seemed
Milestones over the world, and in the sunlight
Their identities oppressed, as all things did
In that meticulous vivisecting light.
Most were anonymous, the scattered ones,
With stones heaped over them to keep their bones
Longer, a little, from jackals and the raven.
'*Ein unbekannter englischer Soldat*'
Held a wild place where there were flowers and larks.
But that was gracious. Most were '*Unbekannt*',
'*Incognito*', 'Unknown'. These haunted most.
For these were us. This was the end we came to,
Whether our bones went underground or not.
Love's individuality became
Ein unbekannter englischer Soldat.
So we despised our bodies, whose too-tired flesh
No longer brought us in its old delights.
And sometimes in the dark, running for shelter,
We stumbled over them, and cursed these dead
Equally with the living, lying still.

JAMES WALKER

The Net Like A White Vault

The net like a white vault, hung overhead
Dewy and glistening in the full moon's light,
Which cast a shadow-pattern of the thread
Over our face and arms, laid still and white
Like polished ivories on the dark bed.
The truck's low side concealed from us the sight
Of tents and bivouacs and track-torn sand
That lay without; only a distant sound
Of gunfire sometimes or, more close at hand,
A bomb, with dull concussion of the ground,
Pressed in upon our world, where, all else banned,
Our lonely souls eddied like echoing sound
Under the white cathedral of the net,
And like a skylark in captivity
Hung fluttering in the meshes of our fate,
With death at hand and, round, eternity.

ENOCH POWELL

Day's Journey

Starting at early light from the old fort
Across the dry flaked mud, you remember,
We left the well on our right and the crosses,
Drove west all day through the camel-scrub,
Tossing in convoy like a mobile orchard,
An olive-yard on wheels, irregular,
Spaced over miles: were bombed: were bombed again,
Until the air was dust: drove on due west

Past the sheikh's tomb of stones, past the dry spring,
Until at dust from the escarpment
Rumbled and boomed the guns' resentment,
Impersonal, the protest of a Titan
Impartially disgusted, while the sun
Signed off in angry flames.
           We halted,
Quietly, in the close leaguer, half ashamed.

                        FRANK THOMPSON
                        killed in action, 1943

Fort Capuzzo

One evening, breaking a jeep journey at Capuzzo,
I noticed a soldier as he entered the cemetery
and stood looking at the grave of a fallen enemy.
Then I understood the meaning of the hard word '*pietas*'
(a word unfamiliar to the newsreel commentator
as well as to the pimp, the informer and the traitor).

His thought was like this. — Here's another 'Good Jerry'!
Poor mucker. Just eighteen. Must be hard-up for Man-power.
Or else he volunteered, silly bastard. That's the fatal,
the — fatal — mistake. Never volunteer for nothing.
I wonder how he died? Just as well it was him, though,
and not one of our chaps. . . , Yes, the only good Jerry,
as they say, is your sort, chum.
                    Cheerio, you poor bastard.
Don't be late on parade when the Lord calls 'Close Order'.
Keep waiting for the angels. Keep listening for Reveille.

                        HAMISH HENDERSON

Lager

I want to effect the retreat of the snail
to drown myself in the sea's sad silence;
I want to effect the mastery of fishes
who travel without star or compass.

I want to forget that the dead are lonely
that the meatless skull has demands on the soil,
has a habit of asking water
with an eye to the growing clover on the chin.

I want to achieve the retreat to the desert
to the vast warmth of illimitable spaces;
I want before morning to make a momentary
reconciliation with silence.

Tomorrow the guns will renew their rumour,
tomorrow the captains will speak with arrows,
tomorrow the duty of battledress blouses
to foster the faces nailed down by death.

But now I want the lament of ocean
which will rest its elbows on upholstered shores
and in secret whisper sadly to the mountains
personal tales of the power of storm.

Now to achieve the retreat of crocus
laying its head in winter's woollen lap
which gathers strength for tomorrow's flowering
tomorrow lifts, grows, splits the earth.

ALAN ROOK

Green, Green Is El Aghir

Sprawled on the crates and sacks in the rear of the truck,
I was gummy-mouthed from the sun and the dust of the track,
And the two Arab soldiers I had taken on as hitch-hikers,
At a torrid petrol-dump, had been there on their hunkers
Since early morning. I said, in a kind of French
'On m'a dit, qu'il y a une belle source d'eau fraîche,
Plus loin, à El Aghir.' It was eighty more kilometres
Until round a corner we heard a splashing of waters,
And there, in a green, dark street, was a fountain with two facets
Discharging both ways, from full-throated faucets
Into basins, thence into troughs and thence into brooks.
Our negro corporal driver slammed his brakes,
And we yelped and leapt from the truck and went at the double
To fill our bidons and bottles and drink and dabble.
Then, swollen with water, we went to an inn for wine.
The Arabs came, too, though their faith might have stood between;
'After all,' they said, 'it's a boisson,' without contrition.

Green, green is El Aghir. It has a railway-station,
And the wealth of its soil has borne many another fruit,
A mairie, a school and an elegant Salle de Fêtes.
Such blessings, as I remarked, in effect, to the waiter,
Are added unto them that have plenty of water.

NORMAN CAMERON

Abruzzi Nightingale

The nightingale will burst his heart
So loudly throbs his bubbling song
This moment in the olive tree,
I listen then I give a start;

For suddenly intrudes a wrong
To Nature – droning from the sea
An enemy bomber clattering
Its strafe-train, unseen, heads this way
To shatter all the joys that sing
Of grief upon the bending spray.

No moon tonight, no trenches dug
No gun emplacement, no tin hat
Just casual irritation's here
To be caught far out from the snug
The usual dug-in habitat,
And suffer more than usual fear.

Ah! but the nightingale he knows
Nothing of how hate hurts the mind
And sings, as bombs crash, to his rose
With note unfaltering, and kind.

JOHN GAWSWORTH

Gallantry

The colonel in a casual voice
spoke into the microphone a joke
which through a hundred earphones broke
into the ears of a doomed race.

Into the ears of the doomed boy, the fool
whose perfectly mannered flesh fell
in opening the door for a shell
as he had learnt to do at school.

Conrad luckily survived the winter:
he wrote a letter to welcome
the suspicious spring: only his silken
intentions severed with a single spinter.

Was George fond of little boys?
we always suspected it,
but who will say: since George was hit
we never mention our surmise.

It was a brave thing the colonel said,
but the whole sky turned too hot
and the three heroes never heard what
it was, gone deaf with steel and lead.

But the bullets cried with laughter,
the shells were overcome with mirth,
plunging their heads in steel and earth –
(the air commented in a whisper).

KEITH DOUGLAS
El Ballah, General Hospital, 1943

Vergissmeinnicht

Three weeks gone and the combatants gone,
returning over the nightmare ground
we found the place again, and found
the soldier sprawling in the sun.

The frowning barrel of his gun
overshadowing. As we came on
that day, he hit my tank with one
like the entry of a demon.

Look. Here in the gunpit spoil
the dishonoured picture of his girl
who has put: *Steffi Vergissmeinnicht*
in a copybook gothic script.

We see him almost with content
abased, and seeming to have paid
and mocked at by his own equipment
that's hard and good when he's decayed.

But she would weep to see today
how on his skin the swart flies move;
the dust upon the paper eye
and the burst stomach like a cave.

For here the lover and killer are mingled
who had one body and one heart.
And death who had the soldier singled
has done the lover mortal hurt.

KEITH DOUGLAS
Homs, Tripolitania, 1943

Landscape With Figures

1

Perched on a great fall of air
a pilot or angel looking down
on some eccentric chart, a plain
dotted with useless furniture,
discerns dying on the sand vehicles
squashed dead or still entire, stunned
like beetles: scattered wingcases and
legs, heads, appear when the dust settles.

But you who like Thomas come
to poke fingers in the wounds
find monuments and metal posies.
On each disordered tomb
the steel is torn into fronds
by the lunatic explosive.

II

On sand and scrub the dead men wriggle
in their dowdy clothes. They are mimes
who express silence and futile aims
enacting this prone and motionless struggle
at a queer angle to the scenery,
crawling on the boards of the stage like walls,
deaf to the one who opens his mouth and calls
silently. The decor is a horrible tracery
of iron. The eye and mouth of each figure
bear the cosmetic blood and the hectic
colours death has the only list of.
A yard more and my little finger
could trace the maquillage of these stony actors:
I am the figure writhing on the backcloth.

Desert Flowers

Living in a wide landscape are the flowers –
Rosenberg I only repeat what you were saying –
the shell and the hawk every hour
are slaying men and jerboas, slaying

the mind: but the body can fill
the hungry flowers and the dogs who cry words
at nights, the most hostile things of all.
But that is not new. Each time the night discards

draperies on the eyes and leaves the mind awake
I look each side of the door of sleep
for the little coin it will take
to buy the secret I shall not keep.

I see men as trees suffering
or confound the detail and the horizon.
Lay the coin on my tongue and I will sing
of what the others never set eyes on.

KEITH DOUGLAS
killed in action, 1944

The Trumpet

O how after Arcturus
have you and your companions
heard the laughter and the distant shout
of the long tube a man sets to his mouth
crying that war is sweet, and the men you
see sleeping after fighting will fight in the day before us?

Since with manual skill
men dressed to kill in purple
with how many strange tongues
cried the trumpet, that cried once
for the death of Hector from Troy steeple
that cried when a hundred hopes fell.

Tonight we heard it
who for weeks have only listened
to the howls of inhuman voices.
But, as the apprehensive ear rejoiced
breathing the notes in, the sky glistened
with a flight of bullets. We must be up early

tomorrow, to forget the cry and the crier
as we forgot the conversation
of our friends killed last month, last week
and hear, crouching, the air shriek
the crescendo, expectancy to elation
violently arriving. The trumpet is a liar.

KEITH DOUGLAS

The Wilderness

I

The red rock wilderness
Shall be my dwelling-place.

Where the wind saws at the bluffs
And the pebble falls like thunder
I shall watch the clawed sun
Tear the rocks asunder.

The seven-branched cactus
Will never sweat wine:
My own bleeding feet
Shall furnish the sign.

The rock says 'Endure'.
The wind says 'Pursue'.
The sun says 'I will suck your bones
And afterwards bury you'.

II

Here where the horned skulls mark the limit
Of instinct and intransigent desire
I beat against the rough-tongued wind
Towards the heart of fire.

So knowing my youth, which was yesterday,
And my pride which shall be gone tomorrow,
I turn my face to the sun, remembering gardens
Planted by others – Longinus, Guillaume de Lorris
And all love's gardeners, in an early May.
O sing, small ancient bird, for I am going
Into the sun's garden, the red rock desert
I have dreamt of and desired more than the lilac's promise.
The flowers of the rock shall never fall.

O speak no more of love and death
And speak no word of sorrow:
My anger's eaten up my pride
And both shall die tomorrow.

Knowing I am no lover, but destroyer,
I am content to face the destroying sun.
There shall be no more journeys, nor the anguish
Of meeting and parting, after the last great parting
From the images of dancing and the gardens
Where the brown bird chokes in its song:
Until that last great meeting among the mountains
Where the metal bird sings madly from the fire.

O speak no more of ceremony,
Speak no more of fame:
My heart must seek a burning land
To bury its foolish pain.

By the dry river at the desert edge
I regret the speaking rivers I have known;
The sunlight shattered under the dark bridge
And many tongues of rivers in the past.
Rivers and gardens, singing under the willows,

The glowing moon . . .
                        And all the poets of summer
Must lament another spirit's passing over.

O never weep for me, my love,
Or seek me in this land:
But light a candle for my luck
And bear it in your hand.

SIDNEY KEYES
killed in action, 1943

The Cruel Sea

Corvette

Dully she shudders at the solid water,
A pause, and spray stings angrily over.
She plunges, and the noisy foam leaps widely
Marbling the moon-grey sea. Loud in the shrouds
Untrammelled winds roar songs of liberty.
Free as the petrels hovering astern
Her long lithe body answers to the swell.

Pardon if all the cleaness and the beauty
Brave rhythm and the immemorial sea
Ensnare us sometimes with their siren song,
Forgetful of our murderous intentions.
Through our uneasy peacetime carnival
Cold sweat of death rained on us like a dew;
Even this grey machinery of murder
Holds beauty and the promise of a future.

NORMAN HAMPSON
H.M.S. Carnation, 1942

Action Stations

'Action stations.' Tin hats and apprehension;
Rush to guns and hoses, engine room
And wireless office. Air of tension.
Eyes uplifted and some seawards gazing.
Ears are straining for a distant 'boom',
Or roar of engines. Lips are phrasing
Prayers, maybe, or curse upon the Hun.
Friendly aircraft in the distance loom
And are gone. Minutes pass . . . 'Carry On'.

JOHN WEDGE

Destroyers In The Arctic

Camouflaged, they detach lengths of sea and sky
When they move; offset, speed and direction are a lie.

Everything is grey anyway; ships, water, snow, faces.
Flanking the convoy, we rarely go through our paces:

But sometimes on tightening waves at night they wheel
Drawing white moons on strings from dripping keel.

Cold cases them, like ships in glass; they are formal,
Not real, except in adversity. Then, too, have to seem normal.

At dusk they intensify dusk, strung out, non-committal:
Waves spill from our wake, crêpe paper magnetised by gun-metal.

They breathe silence, less solid than ghosts, ruminative
As the Arctic breaks up on their sides and they sieve

Moisture into mess-decks. Heat is cold-lined there,
Where we wait for a torpedo and lack air.

Repetitive of each other, imitating the sea's lift and fall,
On the wings of the convoy they indicate rehearsal.

Merchantmen move sideways, with the gait of crustaceans,
Round whom like eels escorts take up their stations.

Landfall, Murmansk; but starboard now a lead-coloured
Island, Jan Mayen. Days identical, hoisted like sails, blurred.

Counters moved on an Admiralty map, snow like confetti
Covers the real us. We dream we are counterfeits tied to our jetty.

But cannot dream long; the sea curdles and sprawls,
Liverishly real, and merciless all else away from us falls.

ALAN ROSS

Naval Base

Waiting in the bar for the war to end –
Those who for the second time saw it begin
And, charting the future, watched death crawling
Like a lizard over the lidless eyes of the sun
And the leprous face of the coast being eaten
Away by the sea – the glass shows them now
The face and features that they find appalling.
Reflections of launches move across the mirror,
Destroyers and corvettes swinging round buoys, sweepers
At anchor – but here the voyages begin and end,
Gin-time stories which they hear, like keepers
Of lightships, as they wait for news of friends –
The same routine, continuing the war until it ends.

ALAN ROSS

Song Of The Dying Gunner

Oh mother my mouth is full of stars
As cartridges in the tray
My blood is a twin-branched scarlet tree
And it runs all runs away.

Oh *Cooks to the Galley* is sounded off
And the lads are down in the mess
But I lie done by the forrard gun
With a bullet in my breast.

Don't send me a parcel at Christmas time
Of socks and nutty and wine
And don't depend on a long weekend
By the Great Western Railway line.

Farewell, Aggie Weston, the Barracks at Guz,
Hang my tiddley suit on the door
I'm sewn up neat in a canvas sheet
And I shan't be home no more.

CHARLES CAUSLEY
on *H.M.S. Glory*

Foreign Commission

November's anger flays all northern seas
And whips great weals across the slaty waste,
The sheering bows fling wide the broken water
It tumbles off the focsles, bitter spray
Knifes by the lively bridges bursting through
And low hulls welter in the marbled water.

On cabin panelling the pictures hold
Their balance in a world swung all awry,
On the damp mess decks now the lisping water
Slides with the restless hours, the cable bangs
Its slow mad rhythm in the naval pipes
And close-packed hammocks jostle all the night.

From heaving tables spins the inky thread
Leading from Theseus through the maze of time
To inland homes where seas are images;
These faded photographs hold frozen truth,
Quick smile, blown hair, in lines map-accurate,
The contour skeleton of living land.

Through all the shapeless months these minds support
Fading perspectives with their wishful dreams,
Assurance grows appeal, their letters scream,
Their own alarm makes fact of all their fear,
The woman's boredom stares between the lines;
And then the silence and the anxious faces.

These are your heroes, whom tomorrow's dawn
May find half-frozen in an oily sea;
They have their memories, their friends who were,
They know the shapes of death and dare forget,
But slow corrosion rusts their lives away
And etches grief on brows that should be young.

There are no killers here, whom crusted pride
Armours against their own humanity,
Or bigot's eyes can blind to bloody hands;
The quiet counties are their pedigree
Whose honest living asks no easy answer
Nor moves the goal to meet their straying ways.

Look for no tragic actors great in stature,
Whose blazing hearts might kindle half a world,
These lives obscure, only their sorrows vast
Winds of humanity that sigh by night
Through all the peopled earth; the men who bear
A fate acceptance cannot make less real.

NORMAN HAMPSON

Home Front

Home Front: 1942

Marching in step, the Battery subalterns
Moving along the footpath of the main road,
Chat about minor military concerns;
Bracing their shoulders as to take a load,
Swinging their canes, eyeing each girl that passes,
Feeling distinctly distant from the masses.

Grudgingly sidecapped gunners give salutes,
Murmur obscenities beneath their breath,
Gossiping news and public house disputes:
Tired of the drag of service, tired to death.
Their only thought to catch a bus as far
As the local town hall dance or cinema.

These carry now the future in the heads
Fouled with the daily drug of great events;
Discuss it in their buttockbiting beds
Or argue in the damp despair of tents
While hired wireless sets dictate aloud
The paths which must be followed by the crowd.

Unheeding now through summer days they give
Their drilled attention to the killers' art
Rehearsing in their minds the life they'll live
When some day soon their second life will start,
And ripping, every time they thrust, the drab,
Embittered present with a bayonet jab.

Sitting in the Mess, the Battery subalterns
Spreading their legs around a firelit hearth,
Distant from Army Orders and returns

Carry their talking down a well trod path.
'When this is finished we'll . . .', is all the theme
Of their age old and never realised dream.

ROBERT L. CHALONER

Rural Sunday

With vacant stare in the market square,
    Tricked out in a lilac suit,
The villager stands with great hands
    And chaffs with a raw recruit.
The heat comes down on a sleepy town
    Like a blanket over the head,
And a church clock beats in the silent streets
    Saying 'Dead, dead, dead'.

The *News of the World* is at last unfurled
    In the strait-lace-curtained window.
Far from the steeple they read in the *People*
    The words of the prophet Lyndoe.
Yesterday's rape was a fine escape
    But today there are tales more thrilling,
Atrocity stories for people whose war is
    A matter of endless killing.

Back from their pews in time for the *News*
    The faithful flock has hastened,
For the polished word of an Oxford Third
    Has left them cheerfully chastened.
Respectable mattins in suits and satins
    Is not for the wretched sinner,
But for those who nod to a friendly God
    And go to a well-cooked dinner.

The flicks are shut and a volunteer hut
    Is the only building alive,
Where a colonel's niece in a smart two-piece
    Serves cups of tea till five.
For those browned-off this attractive toff
    Adds zest to a dreary day,
But the tin doors close and away she goes
    And the world is suddenly grey.

The hour of seven is just like heaven,
    The moment of wishful drinking!
Giggling wenches on bar-room benches
    Can guess what the boys are thinking.
Shropshire lads look a bunch of cads
    As they jingle the week-end cash,
And girls on munitions in certain conditions
    Regret they were once so rash.

Oh, the *Hare and Hounds* may be out of bounds
    To all below the rank of sergeant,
But the bar-maid's charms at the *Talbot Arms*
    Shine gules on a face of argent.
The men say 'cheers' to a round of beers
    And Waafs have a gin and lime,
And the same again till the clock strikes ten
    Saying 'Time, time, time'.

Night must fall but there's nothing at all
    To disturb their accustomed slumber.
They peacefully snore in the midst of war
    An intact and eclectic number.
There comes no ghost to the Warden's Post
    To break the eternal lull,
And to folk like me when the clock strikes three
    It's dull, dull, dull.

                                    MICHAEL BARSLEY

From *Air-Raid Casualties: Ashridge Hospital*

On Sundays friends arrive with kindly words
To peer at those whom war has crushed;
They bring the roar of health into these hushed
And solemn wards –
The summer wind blows through the doors and cools
The sweating forehead; it revives
Memories of other lives
Spent lying in the fields, or by sea-pools;
And ears that can discern
Only the whistling of a bomb it soothes
With tales of water splashing into smooth
Deep rivers fringed with ferns.
Nurses with level eyes, and chaste
In long starched dresses, move
Amongst the maimed, giving love
To strengthen bodies gone to waste.
The convalescents have been wheeled outside,
The sunshine strikes their cheeks and idle fingers,
Bringing to each a sensuous languor
And sentimental sorrow for the dead.

One by one the wards empty, happiness goes,
The hospital routine, the usual work
Return for another week;
The patients turn upon themselves, a hundred foes
Imagined swell their suffering;
Fretfully hands pick at sheets
And voices meet
Discussing symptoms and the chance of living.
Only the soldier lies remote and resolutely sane,

Remembering how, a boy, he dreamt of folk
With footballs. Maturity dispelled the dream – he woke
To know that he would never walk again.

PATRICIA LEDWARD

Officers' Mess

It's going to be a thick night tonight (and the night before was a
                                                    thick one);
I've just seen the Padre disappearing into 'The Cock and Bull'
                                                    for a quick one.
I don't mind telling you this, old boy, we got the Major drinking –
You probably know the amount of gin he's in the habit of sinking –
And then that new M.O. came in, the Jewish one, awful fellow,
And his wife, a nice little bit of stuff, dressed in a flaming yellow.
Looked a pretty warmish piece, old boy – no, have this one with me –
They were both so blind (and so was the Major) that they could
                                                    hardly see.
She had one of those amazing hats and a kind of silver fox fur
(I wouldn't mind betting several fellows have had a go at her).
She made a bee-line for the Major, bloody funny, old boy,
Asked him a lot about horses and India, you know, terribly coy –
And this M.O. fellow was mopping it up and at last he passed
                                                    right out
(Some silly fool behind his back put a bottle of gin in his stout).
I've never seen a man go down so quick. Somebody drove him home.
His wife was almost as bad, old boy, said she felt all alone
And nestled up to the Major – it's a great pity you weren't there –
And the Padre was arguing about the order of morning and
                                                    evening prayer.
Never laughed so much in all my life. We went on drinking till three.
And this woman was doing her best to sit on the Major's knee!

Let's have the blackout boards put up and turn on the other light.
Yes, I think you can count on that, old boy – tonight'll be a
                                                    thick night.

                              GAVIN EWART

Oxford Leave

'The Lamb and Flag' was closed, so I went to the Budolph Hotel
And saw there several faces that I remember too well,
Wartime and peacetime faces, R.A.F. operational types,
Girls who were arty and tarty – and several blokes with pipes.
Young undergraduate faces and over there by the door
Under a smart and once fashionable hat what might (perhaps)
                                                    be a whore.

I stood there like Charles Madge, observing, with the ginger
                                      beer I had bought
(The war had done away with the beer) and to myself I thought
Et ego in Arcadia vixi and worn undergraduate clothes,
No one here is different from me essentially, I suppose, . . .
Plus ça change . . . and a donnish type, a rather middle-aged queen,
Gave me a look, not a dirty look, and I knew what that look could
                                                    mean.

Behind my back was a shocker with a handlebar moustache
Treating a blonde to a *Dubonnet sec* and his laugh was loud and
                                                    harsh.

A rather passé arty woman invited a boy to her home
'We're going to have fish and chips, my dear, really we'ld like
                                      you to come.'
On my left two rich young men were busy discussing the tart,
Two well-fed minds without, I should say, a single constructive
                                                    thought.

Ah, youth! and how time passes! Was it really five years ago
That I left my Alma Mater? Yes, Time is not so slow.
It takes the loves and the parties but nostalgically in the brain
And even in the Army, their memories remain
And these are all real people, not the distortion of dream,
And though one might not believe it, they're all of them what
                                                    they seem.

                              GAVIN EWART

Whit Monday

Their feet on London, their heads in the grey clouds,
The Bank (if you call it a holiday) Holiday crowds
Stroll from street to street, cocking an eye
For where the angel used to be in the sky;
But the Happy Future is a thing of the past and the street
Echoes to nothing but their dawdling feet.
The Lord's my shepherd – familiar words of myth
Stand up better to bombs than a granite monolith,
Perhaps there is something in them. *I'll not want* –
Not when I'm dead. *He makes me down to lie* –
Death my christening and fire my font –
The quiet (Thames' or Don's or Salween's) *waters by*.

                              LOUIS MACNEICE

War Factory

In this imprisoned congo berserk suns
rise with the furnace-doors, make random morn,
set on the molten wave that tideless runs
and from the heat our birds of ice are born.
Here we the oil-black slaves have mastery

creators of the fire and the force
who weave their nests of water and set free
metallic snowbirds, auk and albatross.
Bridled and bitted angels caught in hell,
the endless line of ingots turns and swings
dipping and tossing as our chains compel
till lathe and hammerblow release their wings.
And through cell-windows small we see them fly
the lucid life-and-death way of the sky.

HUBERT NICHOLSON

Cleator Moor

From one shaft at Cleator Moor
They mined for coal and iron ore.
This harvest below ground could show
Black and red currants on one tree.

In furnaces they burnt the coal,
The ore they smelted into steel,
And railway lines from end to end
Corseted the bulging land.

Pylons sprouted on the fells,
Stakes were driven in like nails,
And the ploughed fields of Devonshire
Were sliced with the steel of Cleator Moor.

The land waxed fat and greedy too,
It would not share the fruits it grew,
And coal and ore, as sloe and plum,
Lay black and red for jamming time.

The pylons rusted on the fells,
The gutters leaked beside the walls,
The women searched the ebb-tide tracks
For knobs of coal and broken sticks.

But now the pits are wick with men,
Digging like dogs dig for a bone:
For food and life *we* dig the earth –
In Cleator Moor they dig for death.

Every wagon of cold coal
Is fire to drive a turbine wheel;
Every knuckle of soft ore
A bullet in a soldier's ear.

The miner at the rockface stands,
With his segged and bleeding hands
Heaps on his head the fiery coal,
And feels the iron in his soul.

NORMAN NICHOLSON

The Armoured Valley

Across the armoured valley trenched with light
Cuckoos pump forth their salvoes at the lark,
And blackbirds loud with nervous song and flight
Shudder beneath the hawk's reconnaissance:
Spring is upon us, and our hopes are dark.

For as the petal, and the painted cheek
Issue their tactless beauties to the hour,
We must ignore the budding sun and seek
To camouflage compassion and ourselves
Against the wretched icicles of war.

No festival of love will turn our bones
To flutes of frolic in this month of May,
But tools of hate shall make them into guns
And bore them for the piercing bullet's snout
And through their pipes drain all our blood away.

Yet though by sullen violence we are torn
From violet couches as the air grows sweet,
And by the brutal bugles of retreat
Recalled to snows of death, yet Spring repeat
Your annual attack, pour through the breach
Of some new heart your future victories.

LAURIE LEE

Beneath The German Sky

Oflag Night Piece

There, where the swifts flicker along the wall
And the last light catches – there in the high schloss
(How the town grows dark) all's made impregnable:
They bless each window with a double cross
Of iron; weave close banks of wire and train
Machine guns down them; and look – at the first star
Floodlight the startled darkness back again . . .
All for three hundred prisoners of war.
Yet now past them and the watch they keep,
Unheard, invisible, in ones and pairs,
In groups, in companies – alarms are dumb,
A sentry loiters, a blind searchlight stares –
Unchallenged as their memories of home
The vanishing prisoners escape to sleep.

MICHAEL RIVIERE

The Apple-Trees

There are five apple-trees here, standing in a row:
One day, when the wind began to blow,
   I watched the petals falling
    Into the ditch below.

Beyond the wire is an orchard full of apple-trees:
One morning the petals fallen from these
   Were lying thickly strewn
    Over the grass below.

In my garden in England an apple-tree stands:
Today the petals are fluttering over her hands
   While she is gathering the bluebells
    And the celandines below.

JOHN BUXTON

The Blind Cat

About the Square a black cat plays,
   He has a curious mind,
And lives in a world as dark as himself,
   For this strange black cat is blind.

The black cat goes out to play,
   And men soon gather round
To see him gambol and walk as though
   There are pin-points on the ground.

We all of us like the blind black cat,
   No sister has he or brother;
He was born in the barracks, and lucky for him
   He keeps the love of his mother.

The blind cat's mother, as black as he,
   Parades with her son for play,
She stands on guard with a glint in her eye,
   And frightens the dogs away.

The blind cat's mother, she knows her son
   Can't do his part very well,
So when he goes wrong she calls him home
   To a room where some good men dwell.

Now many of us are like that cat,
   We don't know where we're going.
A pity our mothers are not with us,
   To see what we are doing.

ALEX POTTER

Weltschmerz

Out in the woods the cuckoo
Resounds his note of doom
And the animal evening prowls
At the window of my room.

The trees press in like thunder
Around a rural scene,
Shrieking their dumb-tongued warning
In an agony of green

That plucks at my heart as the tide
Plucks at the lonely stone,
As if her washing kisses
Might cleanse a world of stain,

Where guilt shouts loud from faces
And, far behind the eyes,
The bird-heart beats within its cage
And, inward-turning, dies.

So I who, singing, choose
To be nailed to the living tree
Must key the present to my theme,
Embrace its savagery.

Must outward turn and strip
All armour from my heart
And from the blackthorn's piercing kiss
Turn courage from each hurt.

O animal evening grant me
One all-consuming word;
Strike from my brothers' agony
Such hope as time afford.

ALEXANDER BRYCESON

Second Autumn

So here am I
　　Upon the German earth, beneath the German sky,
　　And birds flock southward, wheeling as they fly,
　　And there are morning mists, and trees turn brown,
　　And the winds blow, and blow the dead leaves down,
　　And lamps are earlier on, and curtains drawn,
　　And nights leave frosted dew-drops on the lawn,
　　And bonfire smoke goes curling up on high,
Just as on English earth, beneath an English sky.
But here am I.

PATRICK SAVAGE

Brief Encounter

Meeting Point

Time was away and somewhere else,
There were two glasses and two chairs
And two people with the one pulse
(Somebody stopped the moving stairs):
Time was away and somewhere else,

And they were neither up nor down,
The stream's music did not stop
Flowing through heather, limpid brown,
Although they sat in a coffee shop
And they were neither up nor down.

The bell was silent in the air
Holding its inverted poise –
Between the clang and clang, a flower,
A brazen calyx of no noise:
The bell was silent in the air.

The camels crossed the miles of sand
That stretched around the cups and plates;
The desert was their own, they planned
To portion out the stars and dates:
The camels crossed the miles of sand.

Time was away and somewhere else.
The waiter did not come, the clock
Forgot them, and the radio waltz
Came out like water from a rock:
Time was away and somewhere else.

Her fingers flicked away the ash
That bloomed again in tropic trees:
Not caring if the markets crash
When they had forests such as these,
Her fingers flicked away the ash.

God or whatever means the Good
Be praised, that time can stop like this,
That what the heart has understood
Can verify in the body's peace
God or whatever means the Good.

Time was away and she was here
And life no longer what it was,
The bell was silent in the air
And all the room aglow because
Time was away and she was here.

LOUIS MACNEICE

Lament

In a dismal air; a light of breaking summer
Under the conspicuous dolour of a leaden sky,
We walk up by the river, beneath the deciduous branches;
Cold in the water the webs of the cold light lie.

Always the sky bleeds with sorrow that no light stanches
In the evenings of autumn, when rust-coloured crisp leaves fly.
Always the heart is uneasy and full of foreboding:
Always the heart is uneasy and cannot tell why.

All the rust of the leaves and the light is corroding
The steel of the evening, gun-metal blue of the sky.
Always the river is lisping and lapping of sorrow.
Like the leaves and the light, the incontinent impulses die.

No more appointments to meet and continue tomorrow,
No more postponements of parting, with hesitant sigh,
Here's the great year in its circle, announcing departure.
Here are your hard lips on mine and goodbye and goodbye.

Summer resumes the occasion but not the adventure.
Always the heart is uneasy and cannot tell why.
In a dismal air; a light of breaking summer,
Cold in the water the webs of the cold light lie.

G. S. FRASER

At The Dark Hour

Our love was conceived in silence and must live silently.
This only our sorrow, and this until the end.
Listen, did we not lie all of one evening
Your heart under my hand.

And no word spoken, no, not even the sighing
Of pain made comfortable, not the heart's beat
Nor sound of urgency, but a fire dying
And the cold sheet?

The sailor goes home singing, the sleepy soldier
May pin to the lit wall his lover's face.
Boys whistle under windows, and are answered;
But we must hold our peace.

Day, too, broke silently. Before the blackbird,
Before the trouble of traffic and the mist unrolled,
I shall remember at the dark hour turning to you
For comfort in the cold.

PAUL DEHN

The Tear

Here in the lounge of this hotel
We struggle for our holy ground,
Our faces play discretion well,
Our deepest anguish breaks no sound;
The spirit's sole confession here
Swims in the crystal of one tear.

We speak; and there is pain in words,
And pain in heart that moves at them;
We splinter mercy into shards,
Yet stoop at once to gather them;
A thousand deaths we take and give,
A thousand deaths that two may live.

If one were evil, one were true,
We should not climb this long distress;
I should destroy the truth in you,
You would corrupt my steadfastness:
Yet here we wrestle, right for right,
As Jacob wrestled, all a night.

Nor you nor I can ever gain
This last decision that we seek,
Your victory will be your pain,
My triumph will be my defeat.
We must now for this logic part,
Twisting the wisdom of the heart.

And yet, this lens of spirit here,
This crystal symbol in your eye,
Denies the images of fear,

Lends faith a new integrity;
In this proud oracle we find
Love neither asks nor grants an end.

Then truth's herself! The lie of fear
Blurs only edges of the mind;
In the swift focus of this tear
Hesitancies of faith have found
Concreteness. Now the ebb of doubt
Runs past the uttermost beaches out.

Now from your soul my eyes remove
One after one each settled mask;
Intuitive fingers of your love
Draw tendrils from my barren dusk:
Truth's inmost curtain opens wide,
And there is no more place to hide.

STEPHEN HAGGARD
Cairo, 1943

Lament

We knelt on the rocks by the dark green pools
The sailor boy and I,
And we dabbled our hands in the weed-veined water
Under a primrose sky.
And we laughed together to hide the sorrow
Of words we left unsaid;
Then he went back to his dirty minesweeper
And I to a lonely bed.
O the anguish of tears unshed.

And never again on this earth shall we meet,
The sailor boy and I,
And never again shall I see his face
Framed in a primrose sky,
For the sea has taken his laughter and loving
And buried him dark and deep
And another lad sleeps on the dirty minesweeper
A sleep that I cannot sleep.
O that I could forget and weep.

FRANCES MAYO

The Meaning Of War

How frequently the last time
Comes and we do not know
That this is indeed the last time
Before all shadows flow
Into a snow of memory
Where memory locks the gates
Of that ice-bound palace garden
Where a few wander like ghosts.

Childhood days by a river
To khaki dreams on a beach
Are usual recollections
That you or I may reach;
But those who deal in hazards
And take what dealing gives
Can never know the last time
In good or fatal moves.

The last time I see people
Is simple as goodbye,
Peter on Weymouth station

Or Kay going home to die.
Goodbye is always a warning
Till the next time we meet
That death is most wary, lurking
Behind unwary feet.

JOHN WALLER

Poem

IV

At main line junctions where such journeys have beginning
Blue tinted partings made we, with hooded trains above us
Hovering and like the fatal cobra hissing.

And we two of two hundred platform lovers
Trundled in wagons, making good our kissing
Until the moving train our parting covers

With the smoke, the garrulous lady, the soldier cursing,
The figure on the platform growing smaller,
And I not daring to withdraw my head lest the women nursing

The sightless child shall offer consolation,
But watch the china potted poles grow taller,
Hearing her sad lips' music in vibration

Of wide-strung wires against the background of the night,
And when at last dry-throated close the window,
To sit cornerwise beneath a smudge of light.

In an aroma of tobacco, sorrow
Collects, as mist about the outer moments of the moon,
And I am left to follow

The katabatic chatter of the train,
And wonder with a calculating eye
Would it be worth five pounds to pull the chain.

GERVASE STEWART
killed in action, 1941

After Several Years

In The Third Year Of War

I dream now of green places,
And the gentle kine
Wading knee-deep in rushes;

I dream of singing birds,
And summer rain,
And gracious, homely words.

But I wake to bitter winds,
And blown sand's whine
Across forgotten lands;

And empty skies at night,
And cold star-shine
Where lonely spirits meet.

I feel all this, my dear,
Alone, my love, alone
With all the old fear.

I dream now there is no ending,
No golden, breathless dawn;
Only seeking, seeking without finding.

HENRY TREECE

After Several Years

The soldier now does not pretend
To more than peace with orders, finds
It easier to be fool friend
Than acid agitator; and so blinds

His eyes to damnfool army things
There is no part of him reminds
Of way that once went upon wings,
Nor laughs at pompous young behinds
Which do not know their cabbages from kings.

The cold insults that snigger at the soul
Are vain to hurt him in his settled years,
For, with the patient nuzzling of a mole,
He burrows past his thoughts of clods and peers
To set himself in some dyspeptic hole
Where nothing will commend, and nothing sneers
And all's as neutral as at some lost pole
Where earth's conflicting dogma disappears.

LAWRENCE LITTLE

The Light Of Day

The light of day is cold and grey and there is no more peace
By the high white moon-washed walls, where we laughed and
where we sung;
And I can't go back to those days of short unthinking ease,
When I was very foolish and you were very young.
For you the laurel and the rose will bloom, and you will see
The dawn's delight, firelight on rafters, wind, seas, and thunder,
Children asleep and dreams and hearts at ease, when life will be,
Even at its close, a quiet and an ageless wonder.
For me the poppies soon will dance and sway in Haute Avesnes:
The sunrise of my love slides into dusk, its day untasted:
Yet as I lie, turf-clad, and freed of passion, and of pain,
I find my sacrifice of golden things not wasted;
Your peace is bought with mine, and I am paid in full, and well,
If but the echo of your laughter reaches me in hell.

DAVID GERAINT JONES
died of wounds, 1944

In Praise Of Home And Rough Weather

Tired and sad, I have of late
Sighed for winter's snow,
To see the cold, grey, listless sky
And the white earth below,
To hear the grass, to hear the trees
Murmuring each to each,
Then moan amidst the driving rain
That lashes on the beach,
And on the hills, and in the lakes,
And through the muddy lanes,
Refreshing now the upturned face,
Now the rich fruitful plains.
Or to return and listen
To winds that murmur low
Across the fields and through the trees
In that land of long ago.
I would lie still and rest there
Amid the scented grass,
And watch, when day is ending,
The purple shadows pass
Across the lonely mountains
That sleep in lands afar,
That loom above the rivers,
That fain would greet a star . . .

The desire to know the thunder,
The snow, the mud, the rain,
Causes my restless spirit
To turn to home again.
Far, far away my heart lies

When the heat is stifling me,
When the rising of the eternal sun
Is life's monotony.

                    DEREK B. READE

Heartbreak Camp

Red as the guardroom lamp
The moon inspects the trees:
High over Heartbreak Camp,
Orion stands at ease:

With buttons lit, for Sentry,
He challenges who's there
Acceding all the entry
Whose passport is Despair.

All joys are privates there
Who seldom go on leave
And only sorrows wear
Three chevrons on their sleeve:

But boredom wears three pips,
A fiend of monstrous size,
With curses on his lips
And circles round his eyes.

All round, for league on league
And labouring up the hills,
The clouds are on fatigue,
Collecting damps and chills.

Sir Dysentery Malaria,
A famous brigadier,
Commands the whole sub-area,
And stalking in his rear,

A more ferocious colonel
Lord Tremens (of the Drunks)
To whose commands infernal
We tremble in our bunks.

Here till the pale aurora
Dismiss the stars from drill,
I dream of my señora
Behind the guardroom grille.

In the outcry of crickets
And the silence of guitars,
I watch the lonely pickets
And the slow patrol of stars.

Our vineyard and the terrace
By the Tagus, they recall,
With the Rose of the Sierras,
Whom I love the best of all!

My heart was once her campfire
And burned for her alone,
Fed with the thyme and samphire
That azure days had grown.

My thoughts for their safari
Have scarcely taken wings
Through spaces wide and starry
To hear her stroke the strings.

But ere one word be spoken
A fiend my elbow jogs,
The reverie is broken
By the tomtom of the wogs:

And, all illusions killing,
Upon the stillness jars
A far hyaena drilling
His company of stars.

ROY CAMPBELL

Mess

How many, before war-ending,
Good or evil winds? –
How many, asked the young captain,
Leaves or wounds?

I had a friend: they
Tore his gentle flesh.
How many, asked the young captain,
Of us will this war finish?

There was a careful silence
After the captain spoke,
Till the Colonel made things decent
With an indecent joke –

And a slightly drunk two-pipper,
Who had travelled in hardware, said:
Better to die living
Than to live dead.

WALTER ANDREWES

War Poet

We in our haste can only see the small components of the scene
We cannot tell what incidents will focus on the final screen.
A barrage of disruptive sound, a petal on a sleeping face,
Both must be noted, both must have their place;
It may be that our later selves or else our unborn sons
Will search for meaning in the dust of long deserted guns,
We only watch, and indicate and make our scribbled pencil notes.
We do not wish to moralize, only to ease our dusty throats.

DONALD BAIN

The Jungle

When you go home
Tell them of us and say
For your tomorrow
We gave our today.

— on the Memorial at Kohima

Disembarkation

Stooping, stumbling, swearing, dull-eyed men
Slouch in long lines across the slippery deck
Emerging slowly from their smelly pen—
Look out there or you'll break your blasted neck! —
And shamble to a blocked companion-way
Where drovers wait to urge them up and on,
While others, from the top, hold them at bay
Until a thousand more have safely gone.
Herded from the ship, they fill the quay
And shuffle into patient, waiting rows,
Helmeted, equipped and blancoed, three by three,
A phalanx dark in which each white face shows:
Then turn and march away who slayed the Hun
To seek the butchers of the Rising Sun.

H. H. TILLEY

Jasper, Marble And Khaki Drill

Incongruous fate for us here to dwell
　　In Khaki commonplace. Silver, exotic
Magenta and gold, disturbing the spell
　　Of our barrack life: entranced, erotic —

Seeming. Thin, strange music, jackals screaming,
　　Sudden, gaudy sundown; turbans, white, and red,
And green; saris, dimness and dreaming;
　　Suburban emotion, rising in bed,

Fearfully painting the innocent drum
　　Of a village wedding feast. Mile End Road

And Norwich, Camberwell, Glasgow and Brum
  Rubbernecking the Taj Mahal (bestowed

By a prince on an unwilling people)
Wishing it were our own church steeple.

REGINALD LEVY

Bengal: After A Storm

Sweetly the sky apologises for
The epileptic interlude, the gibbering rain:
Water in pools shines out like compliments
The reconciling gestures are quite plain
Cool benedictions of the moon
Healing touch of the night air
Cancel our exile and declare
Moment and place are both a boon.
The temporary truce must not deceive;
Already the sneering bull-frog in the slime
And the appalling chorus of jackals
Betray the real intentions of the time.

GEORGE TAYLOR

Forgotten Army

After the heavy heat, the wind came
Fast and hard out of the South,
Destroying sun-drugged moods like flame
Scalding a lotus-oozing mouth.

Wind's lust is strong and male, not hooded
Like the evil of the calm –
A satyr leaping down the wooded slopes,
Raping the naked palm.

Tired bodies stirred then, sensing life,
And raised up languid heads to hear
The long whine like a flying knife
That hits with power, that calls for fear.

Raw violence swept, a cosmic purge
Scouring through decay and rust,
Made blood-mad by deadly surging,
Followed by its jackal – dust.

Hot in the valley curled red smoke,
Choking, blinding, toothed with grit,
While shapeless, mindless sand awoke
And, rabid, tore and clawed and bit.

After the brassy heat, the wind came,
But in the wind the unclean dust,
Until the dust was beaten tame
By rain that swamped the months-old crust.

Beyond the rain, the mud, a vile
Slow worm that fouled the earth
And crushed with hungry, sightless guile
The life that wind had ripped to birth.

The heat – the wind – the dust – the mud
Each grasps its hour, is cut away,
Savaged and slashed within its bud.
But we – we still await our day.

JAMES K. CASSELS

Patrol: Buonomary

Beyond the white dust flushed by the carriers
A scene of mangrove and sea:
Ten small figures running stumbling over the hill,

Our bullets yelping after like harriers
Keen on a kill.

And that was all the enemy's resistance.
The pot-bellied children fondled
Tommy-guns and brens; brought bananas; stared.
The chalk road gashed into the distance,
The sea glared.

The men swam idly all the afternoon,
Beech leaves on the brilliant water;
The tide dropped; stems of the mangroves shiny and seal black
Lifted tight green sheaves from the lagoon;
The horizon went slack

With orange sunset slipping into the sea.
Sentries were detailed and posted.
Night followed the shadows, snakes of fire leapt
Where the men smoked and brewed their tea,
Gossiped and slept.

And in the policeman's house I slowly sipped
The poisonous rhum with some alarm;
Admired a photo of de Gaulle, laboured: '*Oui,
Paris avec les Boches, Madame,
Ce n'est pas Paris.*'

BERNARD GUTTERIDGE

Sniper

Moves in the rocks with inching fingers.
We among the feathery banana trees
Imagine for him his aim: the steel helmet
And English face filling the backsight's V.
Again as it was last time, that spurting noise,
Thud, and the writhing figure in long grass.

Until we match precision with precision:
We move ten men to one and have him then.

I saw the sniper in the afternoon. The rifle
Lay there beside him neatly like his shooting,
The grass twined all about his cap.
He had killed neatly but we had set
Ten men about him to write death in jags
Cutting and spoiling on his face and broken body.

BERNARD GUTTERIDGE

Untitled

Millions of years old – over the whole
Hangs the universe like a dome
Pillared on mountains, that fade into their own height,
Breaking through dense jungle shade to white,
And higher yet into the burning night,
Star-spluttering and belching darkness.
  Over the whole spread a silent vastness
So still, the silence recoiled on itself
And broke to pieces in a myriad whispers –
A mountain stream worming its way to the sea –
The hushed shifting of sand before the breakers,
Heard from miles beyond the forest's edge –
Insects' wings brushing the breathless air –
A leaf falling on leaves and the drip of dew,
Then through the night the howl of homeless dogs
To hurl the stillness back into no noise.
When from the hills, not seen till touching the trees,
Morning, like a flock of flamingoes, wings
To settle in the branches and spread across the fields.

CLIVE BRANSON
killed in action, 1944

Cain In The Jungle

I have killed my brother in the jungle;
Under the green liana's clammy tangle
I hid, and pressed my trigger, and he died.

Smooth as the spotted panther crept my brother,
Never a creak of his equipment's leather,
Never a leaf dislodged nor bird offended.

With his palaeozoic prototype
My mother shared her own ungainly shape
In caverns on some slow Silurian stream;

And with the cublings played my father's sons,
Shoulder to shoulder chipped their flints and bones
Or scraped a greasy ichthyosaurus hide.

And, when the floods of purple slime receded
My brother's hutments by the apes were raided,
I lay beneath my brother's legs and cried.

Yet I have fought my brother for the planets;
I have never stopped to hear the linnets,
Or watch the cocos grow against the moon.

I have only slain him in the shadows,
I have made his slant-eyed women widows
And inherited his empty meadows.

DENYS L. JONES

Observation Post: Forward Area

The thorns are bleached and brittle,
The empty folds decay,
Rooftrees creak in the silence
Of inarticulate dismay.

Drought denudes the planting;
In the dry red heat
Dawn spills its ghostly water,
Black heads on the wheat.

Some evil presence quenches
The vagrant drunken theme
Of the swart and skinny goatherd
And the black goats of his dream.

A darker beast than poverty
Transfixed the crouching peasants there,
And tore the votive tablets down
And filled the children with such fear.

The cowdung fires guttered out,
The wizened women cried,
The bridegroom lay trembling,
And rigid the bride.

Love could be had for nothing.
And where is love now?
Gone with the shambling oxen,
Gone with the broken plough,
Death lives here now.

ALUN LEWIS
died on active service, 1944

Bivouac

There was no trace of heaven
That night as we lay
Punch-drunk and blistered with sunlight
On the ploughed-up clay.

I remember the cactus where our wheels
Had bruised it, bleeding white;
And a fat rat crouching beadyeyed
Caught by my light;

And the dry disturbing whispers
Of the agitated wood,
With its leathery vendetta,
Mantillas dark with blood.

And the darkness drenched with Evil
Haunting as a country song,
Ignoring the protesting cry
Of Right and Wrong.

Yet the peasant was drawing water
With the first excited bird
And the dawn with childish eyes
Observed us as we stirred

And the milk-white oxen waited
Docile at the yoke
As we clipped on our equipment
And scarcely spoke

Being bewildered by the night
And only aware
Of the withering obsession
That lovers grow to fear
When the last note is written
And at last and alone
One of them wakes in terror
And the other is gone.

ALUN LEWIS

From *The Jungle*

I

In mole-blue indolence the sun
Plays idly on the stagnant pool
In whose grey bed black swollen leaf
Holds Autumn rotting like an unfrocked priest.
The crocodile slides from the ochre sand
And drives the great translucent fish
Under the boughs across the running gravel.
Windfalls of brittle mast crunch as we come
To quench more than our thirst – our selves –
Beneath this bamboo bridge, this mantled pool
Where sleep exudes a sinister content
As though all strength of mind and limb must pass
And all fidelities and doubts dissolve,
The weighted world a bubble in each head,
The warm pacts of the flesh betrayed
By the nonchalance of a laugh,
The green indifference of this sleep.

ALUN LEWIS

Into Europe

Calendar Song

The apples I ate in Bedfordshire
    mocked me with red from Alamein
and yellow from sand and the sun that's there
    and green from the wounds in Englishmen.

The leaves that tumbled on Somerset
    like parachutists from a war
brushed down my khaki battle-suit
    shaming my millions everywhere.

The big bare trees in St James's Park
    stretched out their arms like camouflage
and ducks came down like Sunderlands
    and kids pushed off in a landing barge.

I lay by daffodils in Kent
    while men in steel drove up the sky
to toss the earth at an enemy point
    and my colonel said leisurely, by and by.

But O, when they woke me up in June
    and told all thumbs to touch the news
I heard my boats grind into France
    and the prisoning seasons let me loose.

ARNOLD RATTENBURY

A Minor Front

The bridge attributed to Belisarius
Is blown, and we cross the stream on foot
Towards the little town.

> Absolute power
Has receded like a tide from the Thracian hills
And the people reappears, a streaming rock
Surrounded by dead monsters.
> Across the Struma
The German outposts can be seen, and their patrols
Still cross the river almost unopposed.
For the retreat was caused by pressure elsewhere
And here no force of partisans can yet
Resist them. Half a dozen towns
Still lie in a no-man's land which small patrols
Alone can enter.
> The clouds appear
Fully created in the Aegean sky
And ahead of us the stony and half-empty
Struma glistens.
> Among the buildings
(Not too badly wrecked) people are moving.
An old man, carrying a wooden bucket
Full of goat's milk, staggers to his neighbour's.
– The quick withdrawal of that violent empire
Has left a vacuum of rule. Government is dead;
And after the executions by patrols the tired survivors
Learn, for a few days, to work together, to live.
The best are in the mountains with the partisans
Or rotting in Salonika jail. The worst come out
To loot or denounce. And among the others only,
Mediocre and stupid, in small and selfish cities,
Half-suffocated by starvation and disease,
The free life of the holiday camp arises.
Very dimly through a host of more immediate noises
They faintly hear the music of the stateless future
Like a distant waterfall.
> But there is too much.
Too much confusion! Too much metal!

They have gazed too long into a mirror of Europe
And seen the Minotaur reflections gnash their teeth,
And they cannot keep their eyes on the green star
Nor listen to the bells.
                  The sky glitters, burning coldly.
The moment is losing its illumination;
The world of politics and rifles reappears;
In Seres, Drama, Sidhirokastron, life will revert
To the visionless present.
                We lower our field-glasses,
And walk back to the far end of the village,
And pull out our rations and begin to eat,
As by the failing light we try to interpret
The gilt inscription on the public monument
In front of which, their hands still tied behind them,
The bodies of two gendarmes lie in the street.

ROBERT CONQUEST

Steep Stone Steps

Steep stone steps, stinking with washing water,
Italy inhales its incense, Dante's derelict daughter.
Poverty, Peter's Pence, politics, capital, conniving
Thieves thwart the thankless struggler's stalwart striving;
Hard, hoarding husbandry doomed, daunted, defeated,
Master masons, metalworkers chidden, checked, cheated.
Rich rogues revel, frauds fatten. What wonder
Dignity departs, patriotism perishes, petty plunder,
Servile subterfuges spread social suppuration?
Nevertheless nature's high heart carries consolation:
Generosity, joy, gentleness, mankind's measureless mines,
Love, laughter lavishly live, sun shines.

NORMAN CAMERON

War Dead

With grey arm twisted over a green face
The dust of passing trucks swirls over him,
Lying by the roadside in his proper place,
For he has crossed the ultimate far rim
That hides from us the valley of the dead.
He lies like used equipment thrown aside,
Of which our swift advance can take no heed,
Roses, triumphal cars – but this one died.

Once war memorials, pitiful attempt
In some vague way regretfully to atone
For those lost futures that the dead had dreamt,
Covered the land with their lamenting stone –
But in our hearts we bear a heavier load:
The bodies of the dead beside the road.

GAVIN EWART
near La Spezia, April 1945

The Guardsman

His eyes were closed. Against his will he'd dared
A dreadful danger, one that all had shared,
But he had simply died. The fretful throes
Of killing now were quiet in those rows
Of strangely ugly men, so loath to send
The struggle for existence from their hand.
Uncovered his face had mustered silence
And the bitterness of all ignorance,
And I did not see the slightest glory

Reflected in that flesh so old and grey.
He was quite dead and yet I could not shed
Tears, it was so earthly and expected,
And it seemed clear that he would have to wake,
Inevitably, as usual, at break
Of dawn somewhere, fed up, courageous, vain
As ever, swear and start it all again.

G. A. WAGNER

After Night Offensive

Glowed through the violet petal of the sky
Like a death's-head the calm summer moon
And all the distance echoed with owl-cry.

Hissing the white waves of grass unsealed
Peer of moon on metal, hidden men,
As the wind foamed deeply through the field.

Rooted to soil, remote and faint as stars,
Looking to neither side, they lay all night
Sunken in the murmurous seas of grass.

No flare burned upwards: never sound was shed
But lulling cries of owls beyond the world
As wind and moon played softly with the dead.

JAMES FARRAR
killed in action, 1944

St Aubin D'Aubigné

It was only a small place and they had cheered us too much,
A couple of allies, chance symbol of Freedom new-found.
They were eager to beckon, to back-slap, even to touch;
They put flowers in my helmet and corn-coloured wine in my hand.

The boy from Dakota and I, we had suffered too little
To deserve all the flowers, the kisses, the wine and the thanks.
We both felt ashamed; till the kettledrum clangour of metal
On cobble and kerbstone proclaimed the arrival of tanks.

Who saw them first, the exiles returning, the fighters,
The Croix de Lorraine and the Tricolour flown from the hull?
Who saw us moving more fitly to join the spectators,
The crazy, the crying, the silent whose hearts were full?

It was only a small place, but a bugle was blowing.
I remember the Mayor performing an intricate dance
And the boy from Dakota most gravely, most quietly, throwing
The flowers from his helmet toward the deserving of France.

PAUL DEHN
August 1944

Victoria Leave Train

In the sixth year faces are as tense as ever,
Lit up in the crowded train on the return journey,
My Generation death-image-haunted as in a fever.

Homesickness sprawls on packs with a sad sleepy smile,
Red flashes of courage, echoes of fading adventures,
Bother the Midnight subconscious as mile on mile

A flush of correspondents sit like migrating swallows
Unaware of the mapped forest and the assembled shallows
Watching the beginning of one more trip to the End.

From the tossing, the lolling bodies of early morning
Lingering in files, from the assembled derisive sneer
Comes no sense of Identification and certainly no singing.

For them it's loudspeaker directions under the electric glare,
A second hard embarkation bereft of many a luckless friend.
Soldiers with families O who pities you as you were?

You boarded the Ship whose decks were swept, you slept
Outside cabins; or changed your money with sore heart
Expecting to go every minute expecting the show to start.

Yet you never grumbled like a second line draft
Back beyond A Echelon; so if there are saints aboard
Let them send up their complaints like a thunderclap to heaven.

And will the soldier who brought back a model last week
Of a Spanish galleon as a present go to ship's deck forward
If he is aboard.

Waiting, waiting, it is always waiting around
For something to happen, for the issue to be decided.

Resigned – these are not glory-fed, have no illusions.
Remember the cinnamon dusty of Normandy, their
                                    booby-trapped dead.
And they also know the despair of battles won.

For only the Fortunate
Will ever run the gauntlet of the queue's eager
Questioning eyes at Victoria again.

KEIDRYCH RHYS

Memento

Remember the blackness of that flesh
Tarring the bones with a thin varnish
Belsen Theresenstadt Buchenwald where
Faces were a clenched despair
Knocking at the bird-song-fretted air.

Their eyes sunk jellied in their holes
Were held up to the sun like begging bowls
Their hands like rakes with finger-nails of rust
Scratched for a little kindness from the dust.
To many, in its beak, no dove brought answer.

STEPHEN SPENDER

Stateless Persons

They carry no shadow in sunlight, the past like a slate
Rubbed out on a future that arrived too late.

Their faces are maps of a landscape, whose ghosts hover
Around them, an arena of ruins that are all like each other.

And their words are a Babel whose meaning is plain —
The shadow of Cain has been thrown on to Abel.

So, unseen, the derelict cities crowd in on their eyes;
But self-pity has grown and conditioned surprise.

Now nothing is important, enormous or true. The message
Was too long delayed; they are part of their passage.

The long shadow has turned into stone, the pillar grown salt
Not a wife. And Death, too, is over, like life.

ALAN ROSS

Midnight: May 7th, 1945

Thunder gathers all the sky,
Tomorrow night a war will end,
Men their natural deaths may die
And Cain shall be his brother's friend.

From the lethal clouds of lead
Thickening hatred shall descend
In fruitful rain upon the head:
Tomorrow night a war will end.

Thunder, mock not Abel's cry:
Let this symbolic storm expend
The sum of man's malignity!
– And Cain shall be his brother's friend.

There are no words to be said:
Let the future recommend
The living to the luckless dead.
Tomorrow night a war will end.

PATRIC DICKINSON

Victory

The Voyage Back

It was the time of voyaging back. It was the time, now, at last.
We had come to the end of the days and nights we went patrolling
The wastes of ocean. We'll not retrace our wake, all that is past;
The salt-bleached struggling ship, the frozen spray in the rigging,
Like filigree icing, and the sight of seamen's wind-scored faces
As they hump the shells, with blue-red hands, to the taut, whitened,
Intractable single-whip tackle while the ship plunges and races,
Shudders and slips to the slash of the waves, and the stomach
                                        feels tightened
In a gritted, queasy contraction, and the smell from the galley
Swims in the head, and the staler stench of tobacco smoke stains
Fingers and mouth. To watch no more for the green break of
                                        light that stilly
Creeps out of the spume to etch again the twisted convoy lanes,
And later the stretched off stragglers hove up from the pallid mouth
Of a snowing dawn. To feel, to know, to touch this no more,
To say it is done, for a few years at least, makes the heart want to
                                        shout
With the joy of relief for the flesh that was flayed by the raw
Wracking winds from the south and the west. Praise God,
                                        it was the last, last time;
We were just about at the end of the rope, waking or sleeping,
We dreamed of the plunge and the rise and the endless wind and the
                                        rime
Of the needling frost that ate its way into eyes and ears and brain.
No wonder I saw a young seaman his face puckered and weeping
As we ran in the lee of the land back to port and he felt the rain
Falling quietly down from a sky that stood still, out of a peace
That spelled home, gentleness, love. His tears were only the tears
                                        of release.

R. C. M. HOWARD
Far East, August 1945

Hats, Demob Depot, York

Arriving at a counter heaped with hats,
'Here comes another head,' thought I. 'So shrinks
Their number as more heads approach, and we
Don our old differences, hat by hat.
A hideous journey brings us to this halt.
How many have dropped out! The rest, once more
Parading, take their choice, then finally
Diverge into the oblivion of freedom.'

But suddenly, before we went our ways,
The clear impression of another hour
Flashed on the mind. There was a thoroughfare
Of waving hands, flags, handkerchiefs, and hats,
And all the windows weeping paper tears,
Weeping waste paper for the wasted years.

CHRISTOPHER HASSALL

Armistice

Now the lost traveller, with sun-bleached hair
Dazed on the gangway, shall come home again,
The end is changed; it is no more despair,
Nor the gashed limbs rolled shorewards by the tide,
But sirens booming through the harbour air
And all the applauding windows opened wide,
For Birnam Wood has marched to ransom Dunsinane.

Now friends who locked their hopes to be restored
Each to the other's world-creating smile
Below the hatches of their hearts to hoard,

While the ill dream was of divided graves,
Desert or jungle, and the tempest roared,
Clasp their reunion in this hour that saves
Under the blossom that hangs on the enchanted isle.

Reunion and reprieve: the words like suns
Blaze on the day these garland bells acclaim,
And the great axle of doom that seemed to run
Backwards for ever to the unlucky dead
Palpable over them as tank or gun,
Dissolves in mist beneath those words instead –
See: the veiled statue wakes, resumes her breathing name.

The soldier drops his weapons at the door
And from his forehead wipes the brand of Cain,
The toasts are raised, the dancing shakes the floor,
And that tall stranger with the eyes of ice –
Look round, and laugh, for he is there no more
To drain the tankard with the skull device –
For the green springing host has come to Dunsinane.

JOHN LEHMANN

Victory

Tempest and flood,
Rats in the granary, the maggot coiled
Within the bud,
All summer's teeming promise wrecked and spoiled,
This is our lot.
Our farms decay, the acres that we cherish
Consume with rot;
Our children, like our flocks, grow thin and perish.
The smallest shower

Plucks off the unripe plum, the frailest weed
    Drags down the flower:
Now only dock and darnel bear their seed.
    And how, when storm
Already quenches autumn's guttering ember,
    Shall we keep warm
Through the long polar nightmare of December?
    Are these the yields
For which with so much hope and so much labour
    We fenced our fields
And slew the servants of our jealous neighbour?
    . . . Meanwhile, like crows,
Our three old landlords sit and quarrel
    For a dead rose
And a few sheaves of thistle, rue and sorrel.

FRANCIS KING

Poem After Victory

Counting his dead in the morning, he discovers
    The brilliant legions of passion lying slain,
And now returning the worn uncertain survivors:
    Pity and grief and pain.

Remembered grief may people the desolate city,
    And the severed limbs will be reshaped in pain;
But useless for now is the shattered stump of pity
    Bleeding within his brain.

Nor for some time will the prisoned words be calling
    Or the waves of feeling beat on the walls of the brain:
For the storm is over; the last emotions are falling
    Characterless as rain.

Is black and stagnant his soul, receiving and giving
  Nothing: swollen with truth as the gutters with rain:
And corpses exhale no pity; and the living
  Batten upon the slain.

JOHN R. TOWNSEND

Song

  Sailor, harrowing the seas,
  Your eyebrows caked with salt
  No harbour siren's kiss
  Shall ever melt.

  Soldier, snatching the bitter
  Open-mouthed sleep,
  For you the cosy taproom
  No refreshment keeps.

  Airman, down to earth,
  Painting the town red,
  Swingbands merely enlarge the hollow
  Singing in your head.

  And your hearths shall be baffled, wherever
  You settle, north or south,
  By that airy keening, stiff alien
  Salt, and the gall in your mouth.

GORDON SYMES

Walking Wounded

A mammoth morning moved grey flanks and groaned.
In the rusty hedges pale rags of mist hung;
The gruel of mud and leaves in the mauled lane
Smelled sweet, like blood. Birds had died or flown,
Their green and silent attics sprouting now
With branches of leafed steel, hiding round eyes
And ripe grenades ready to drop and burst.
In the ditch at the cross-roads the fallen rider lay
Hugging his dead machine and did not stir
At crunch of mortar, tantrum of a Bren
Answering a Spandau's manic jabber.
Then into sight the ambulance came,
Stumbling and churning past the broken farm,
The amputated sign-post and smashed trees,
Slow wagonloads of bandaged cries, square trucks
That rolled on ominous wheels, vehicles
Made mythopoeic by their mortal freight
And crimson crosses on the dirty white.
This grave procession passèd, though, for a while,
The grinding of their engines could be heard,
A dark noise on the pallor of the morning,
Dark as dried blood; and then it faded, died.
The road was empty, but it seemed to wait –
Like a stage which knows the cast is in the wings –
Wait for a different traffic to appear.
The mist still hung in snags from dripping thorns;
Absent-minded guns still sighed and thumped.
And then they came, the walking wounded,
Straggling the road like convicts loosely chained,
Dragging at ankles exhaustion and despair.
Their heads were weighted down by last night's lead,

And eyes still drank the dark. They trailed the night
Along the morning road. Some limped on sticks;
Others wore rough dressings, splints and slings;
A few had turbanned heads, the dirty cloth
Brown-badged with blood. A humble brotherhood,
Not one was suffering from a lethal hurt,
They were not magnified by noble wounds,
There was no splendour in that company.
And yet, remembering after eighteen years,
In the heart's throat a sour sadness stirs;
Imagination pauses and returns
To see them walking still, but multiplied
In thousands now. And when heroic corpses
Turn slowly in their decorated sleep
And every ambulance has disappeared
The walking wounded still trudge down that lane,
And when recalled they must bear arms again.

VERNON SCANNELL

Epilogue

The Shadow Of Cain

Two Extracts

We did not heed the Cloud in the Heavens shaped like the hand
Of man ... But there came a roar as if the Sun and Earth had
come together –
The Sun descending and the Earth ascending
To take its place above ... the Primal Matter
Was broken, the womb from which all life began,
Then to the murdered Sun a totem pole of dust arose in memory
of Man.

*　　*　　*

There are no thunders, there are no fires, no suns, no earthquakes
Left in our blood. .... But yet like the rolling thunders of all
the fires in the world, we cry
To Dives: 'You are the shadow of Cain. Your shade is the primal
Hunger.'
'I lie under what condemnation?'
'The same as Adam, the same as Cain, the same as Sodom,
the same as Judas.'

And the fires of your Hell shall not be quenched by the rain
From those torn and parti-coloured garments of Christ, those rags
That once were Men. Each wound, each stripe,
Cries out more loudly than the voice of Cain –

Saying 'Am I my brother's keeper?' Think! When the last clamour
of the Bought and Sold
The agony of Gold
Is hushed, ... When the last Judas-kiss

Has died upon the cheek of the Starved Man Christ, these ashes
that were Men

Will rise again
To be our Fires upon the Judgment Day,
And yet – who dreamed that Christ has died in vain?
He walks again on the Seas of Blood, He comes in the terrible Rain.

EDITH SITWELL

Biographies

Biographies

* Died on Active Service

*DRUMMOND ALLISON (East Surrey Regiment). Born in 1921, at Caterham, Surrey. Educated: Bishop's Stortford, and Queen's College, Oxford. Sandhurst, 1942. School of Military Engineering, 1943. Served in North Africa and Italy. Killed in action on the Garigliano, Italy, on December 2, 1943. Allison's poems were collected in 1944.

KENNETH ALLOTT. Born in 1912. Educated: Durham and Oxford Universities. Associated with *New Verse* before the war; Allott's first volume of poems was published in 1938. Biographer, poet and critic. University lecturer after the war. 'Ragnarok' is a Scandinavian legend telling of the destruction of the world.

*BRIAN ALLWOOD (R.A.F.). Born in 1920. Allwood worked with Mass Observation before the war. He joined the Air Force in 1941, was married in September of the following year, and eight weeks later was sent to North Africa. He was mentioned in despatches, June 1943. The poems reprinted here were first published in a *Resurgam* broadsheet. Allwood was also published in *More Poems from the Forces* in 1943. He was killed in Italy on June 30, 1944, and is buried at Caserta.

WALTER ANDREWES (Army). Born in 1913. Educated: Canford, and Keble College, Oxford. Editor of *Isis*. Literary agent before the war. Andrewes was at Dunkirk; later he was made a Staff Captain. 'Mess' was first published in *Penguin New Writing*, 1943.

JOHN ARLOTT. Born in 1914, at Basingstoke. Educated: Queen Mary's School, Basingstoke. Police Force before and during the war. His *Clausentum*, from which 'The Bomb Crater' is taken, is about a place of habitation for two thousand years disrupted by the Blitz. Broadcaster, and writer on cricket.

W. H. AUDEN. Born in 1907. Educated: Gresham's School, and Christ Church, Oxford. Stretcher-bearer in Spanish Civil War. Auden's residence in the United States was the cause of controversy in 1940; it was the subject of a Question in the House of Commons, June 13, 1940. Auden had in fact undertaken to return to Britain if called upon to do so. He served with the Strategic Bombing Survey of the U.S. Army in Germany.

BRUCE BAIN (R.A.F.). Born 1921, in London. The two poems reprinted here first appeared in *Poets Now*, No. 2, published by the Favil Press. Bruce Bain was also published in *More Poems From The Forces*. Later journalist, critic, and author (Richard Findlater).

DONALD BAIN (Royal Artillery, and Gordon Highlanders). Born in 1922, at Liverpool. Educated: King's College, Cambridge. Invalided out before the end of the war, Bain took up an acting career. Contributor to *Penguin New Writing*, and co-editor of *Oxford and Cambridge Writing*, 1942.

PETER BAKER (Royal Artillery). Born in 1921. Baker was about to enter Trinity College, Cambridge, when war was declared; he enlisted instead. 'Epilogue' was first published in *Resurgam*, No. 1, by the Favil Press. Captain; M.C; captured by the Gestapo. Publisher and M.P. after the war. Died in 1966.

GEORGE BARKER. Born 1913, in Essex. Educated: L.C.C. School in Chelsea, and Polytechnic. Barker was a Professor of English Literature in Japan at the outbreak of war. He went to the

United States, and returned to Britain in 1943. His first book of poems was published in 1933.

MICHAEL BARSLEY. Born in 1913. He began the war as a Conscientious Objector, but became disillusioned with pacifism. The poem here was written in 1941, when he was a farm worker in the Midlands. It appeared in *Horizon*, November 1942. Barsley became an ambulance driver in London. After the war: author.

JOHN BAYLISS (R.A.F.). Born 1919, in Gloucestershire. Educated: Latymer Upper, and St Catharine's College, Cambridge. Flight Lieutenant. Editor and poet of the war years. Co-editor of *New Road*, 1943–44, with Alex Comfort. 'Reported Missing' was published in *Air Force Poetry*, 1944. Worked in publishing and Civil Service after the war, in London and Africa.

D. van den BOGAERDE (Queen's Royal Regiment). Born in 1921. Educated: University College School, and Allan Glen's School. Served in Europe and the Far East. 'Steel Cathedrals' was first published in *Poetry Review*, 1943. Bogaerde also had war poetry in *The Times Literary Supplement*. After the war: film actor (Dirk Bogarde).

*DAVID BOURNE (R.A.F.). Born in 1921, at Meopham, Kent. Educated: Cranbrook. Pilot Officer, R.A.F.V.R. Bourne left about 140 poems of which nearly half were collected and published by the Bodley Head in 1944. He was shot down and killed on September 5, 1941.

*CLIVE BRANSON (Royal Armoured Corps). Born 1907, in India. Educated: Bedford, and Slade School of Art. Fought in Spain, where he was captured and spent eight months in a prison camp. Exhibitor at the Royal Academy. Killed in action on the Arakan front, February 25, 1944. The poem reprinted here was written a few days before his death: 'I am on guard again tonight and it is very cold. This last few minutes I have been writing these lines.'

J. BRONOWSKI. Born in 1908. Educated: Central Foundation School, London, and Jesus College, Cambridge. Scientist, and authority on William Blake; a collection of his poetry was published in 1939. Served with Joint Target Group, Washington, and Chiefs of Staff Mission, Japan. Director of National Coal Board Research Establishment, 1950–60; radio and television broadcaster.

JOCELYN BROOKE (Royal Army Medical Corps). Born in 1908, at Sandgate, Kent. Educated: Bedales, and Worcester College, Oxford. Brooke served in several theatres, including North Africa and Italy. After the war: author. First volume of poetry published in 1946. Died in 1966.

ALEXANDER BRYCESON (R.A.F.). Born in 1919. Educated: Magdalene College, Cambridge. Bryceson was shot down over Germany, early in 1941, and spent four-and-a-half years in a number of prison camps. 'Weltschmerz' appeared in *Poetry From Cambridge in Wartime*, edited by Geoffrey Moore, 1946.

JOHN BUXTON (No. 1 Independent Company). Born 1912, in Cheshire. Educated: Malvern, and New College, Oxford. Buxton, a pre-war poet, was taken prisoner in Norway, in the spring of 1940, and interned in *Oflag VII*. A collection of his poems from Germany was published by Macmillan in 1944.

NORMAN CAMERON (Intelligence). Born 1905, in India. Educated: Fettes, and Oriel College, Oxford. An advertising copy-writer with J. Walter Thompson before the war, and poet. For his work in political intelligence and propaganda during the war, Cameron was awarded the M.B.E. Died in 1953.

ROY CAMPBELL (King's African Rifles). Born 1901, in South Africa. Educated: Durban High School. Pre-war poet; lived in France, Portugal and Spain, where he was not unknown as a bull-fighter and steer-thrower. Fought in Spain – on Franco's side, unlike other poets. Served in North and East Africa as Sergeant until invalided out in 1944. Died in motor accident, 1957.

JAMES K. CASSELS (Army). Born 1909, in Scotland. Edu-cated: Edinburgh University. Teacher, and studied for ordination before the war. At Dunkirk; later served in South East Asia; Parachute 'wings'; West African Signals. Minister in Church of Scotland.

CHARLES CAUSLEY (Royal Navy). Born in 1917, at Launces-ton, Cornwall. Educated: Horwell Grammar School, and Peter-borough Training College. In the Navy from 1940 to 1946, mostly with the Communications Branch. Orkneys, Atlantic, Gibraltar. Teacher, poet and broadcaster. With B.B.C. 1953–56. Causley's first volume of poetry was published in 1951.

ROBERT L. CHALONER (Royal Artillery). Born in 1916. Educated: Jesus College, Oxford. Captain, Medium Artillery from Caen to Hamburg. After the war: journalist.

ROBERT CONQUEST (Ox. & Bucks. Light Infantry). Born in 1917, at Malvern. Educated: Winchester, and Magdalen College, Oxford. Served in Bulgaria and the Ukraine. In Diplomatic Service after the war: Balkans, United Nations. Poet, literary journalist, and writer on Russian affairs. First volume of poetry published in 1955.

HERBERT CORBY (R.A.F.). Born 1911, in London. Served as an Armourer in a bomber squadron, working on Hampdens and Lancasters, and then as an Armaments Instructor. He was repre-sented in *Best Poems of 1942*, and his war poetry was collected in 1945 and 1947. In the Foreign Service after the war.

*JOHN CORNFORD. Born in 1915, and christened Rupert John after Rupert Brooke, who had just died, a friend of his parents. His mother was poet Frances Cornford, and his father a professor. Educated: Stowe, and Trinity College, Cambridge (to which he won an Open Major Scholarship at the age of sixteen). After a brilliant start to an academic career, he joined the Communist Party, went to Spain, and was killed by machine-gun fire the day after his twenty-first birthday.

*TIMOTHY CORSELLIS (R.A.F.). Born in 1921. Educated: Winchester. In A.R.P. during the London Blitz. A friend of the R.A.F. poet Nigel Weir, q.v., on whose death in action Corsellis wrote his last published poem. Served for a time as a 2nd Officer in the Air Transport Auxiliary. Contributor to *More Poems from the Forces* and *Poems of This War*. Died in action, 1941.

R. N. CURREY (Royal Artillery, and Army Educational Corps). Born 1907, in South Africa. Educated: Kingswood, and Wadham College, Oxford. Schoolmaster before the war. Joined the Army in 1941, and was posted to India in 1943. Rose to the rank of Major. War poetry collected by Routledge in 1945. Author of *Poets of the 1939–45 War*, 1960. Schoolmaster.

C. DAY LEWIS. Born in 1904, near Sligo, in Ireland. Educated: Sherborne, and Wadham College, Oxford. Edited *Oxford Poetry* with Auden in 1927. Associated with Auden, Christopher Isherwood, MacNeice, and Stephen Spender, in the pre-war decade. Schoolmaster before the war. Ministry of Information, 1941–46. Poet, and writer of detective novels. Professor of Poetry, Oxford, 1951–56.

PAUL DEHN (London Scottish, and Intelligence Corps). Born in 1912. Educated: Shrewsbury, and Brasenose College, Oxford.

Film critic before the war. Reached the rank of Major as an instructor with S.O.E. After the war: script-writer, librettist, and film critic. Poems collected in 1965.

PATRIC DICKINSON (Artists' Rifles). Born 1914, in India. Educated: St Catharine's College, Cambridge. Golf blue. After the war: poet, critic and broadcaster. First book of poetry published in 1946.

*KEITH DOUGLAS (Sherwood Rangers Yeomanry). Born in 1920, at Tunbridge Wells. Educated: Christ's Hospital, and Merton College, Oxford. He won all his education by scholarship, and was writing talented poetry by the age of sixteen, when he was first published. Editor of *Cherwell*. Fought in a Crusader tank from Alamein to Tunisia, apart from one spell when he was wounded by a mine. Author of *Alamein to Zem-Zem*, a prose account of tank warfare in the desert. Arranged for the publication of his poetry before D-Day: 'I cannot afford to wait, because of military engagements which may be the end of me.' Promoted to Captain. Killed by enemy artillery fire on his third day in Normandy, June 9, 1944.

GAVIN EWART (Royal Artillery). Born in 1916. Educated: Wellington, and Christ's College, Cambridge. In advertising and literary work before the war. Officer in the R.A.: North Africa, Italy. Ewart had already had a book of verse published by the start of the war. Contributor to leading publications since his schooldays. 'Officers' Mess' was first published in *Horizon*, 1942.

*JAMES FARRAR (R.A.F.). Born 1923, at Woodford, Essex. Educated in Sutton, Surrey. At the start of the war he worked on a farm in Cornwall, and joined up in 1942. He lost his life in a Mosquito aircraft on July 26, 1944, while attacking a V-1 flying bomb. Farrar was first published in *The Adelphi*. A Collection of his poems and miscellaneous writings was published in 1950, edited by

Henry Williamson, who said: 'had he lived he would undoubtedly have risen to a high place as a novelist and writer'.

*KEITH FOOTTIT (R.A.F.). Born 1922, in India. Educated: Wellington. Awarded an Exhibition to Brasenose College, Oxford, but joined the Air Force. Trained in the United States; Flying Officer; pilot of a Halifax bomber. Represented in *For Your Tomorrow*, 1950. He was killed when his aircraft was shot down over Magdeburg, January 21, 1944. Poems collected in 1948.

G. S. FRASER (Black Watch, and R.A.S.C.). Born 1915, in Glasgow. Educated: Aberdeen Grammar School, and St Andrew's University. Journalist before the war. Rose in Middle East from rank of Private to W.O.2. Worked for some time on a Forces newspaper in East Africa. After the war: writer and university lecturer. Two volumes of war poetry: in 1944, and 1947.

DAVID GASCOYNE. Born in 1916. Educated: Salisbury Cathedral Choir School, and Regent Street Polytechnic. Gascoyne had published a volume of poetry and a novel by the age of seventeen. Before the war he lived for a time in France, and did some translation. Poems collected in 1965.

JOHN GAWSWORTH (R.A.F.). Born 1912, in London. Educated: Merchant Taylors'. Founder-editor of *The English Digest*, and leader of the neo-Georgian movement of the late 1930s. Seven volumes of poetry published by 1945. Served in North Africa, Italy, and India, becoming a Flying Officer.

BERNARD GUTTERIDGE (Hampshire Regt.). Born in 1916, at Southampton. Educated: Cranleigh. Bernard Gutteridge was in advertising before the war. He served in Combined Operations and with the 36th Division in Burma (with Alun Lewis), reaching the rank of Major. 'Buonomary' was written in Madagascar.

Contributor to the leading periodicals. War poems collected in 1947.

*STEPHEN HAGGARD (Devonshire Regt., and Intelligence Corps). Born 1911, in New York, son of the British Consul-General, and a descendant of Rider Haggard. Educated: Hailey-bury, and Munich University. Notable theatre and film actor before the war, and also author. Staff Captain. Shot mysteriously in train from Jerusalem to Cairo, February 24, 1943, leaving two sons. Haggard's biography, by Christopher Hassall, was published in 1948.

CHARLES HAMBLETT (R.A.F.). Born in Lancashire. Educated: Vienna, and at the School of Arts and Crafts, Cambridge. Contributed to a number of periodicals during the war. After the war he became a journalist based on Hollywood. A collection of his war and other poems was published in 1946.

MICHAEL HAMBURGER (Army). Born 1924, in Berlin. Educated: Westminster, and Christ Church, Oxford. In the Army 1943–47. Afterwards, poet and university lecturer. First volume of poetry published in 1950.

NORMAN HAMPSON (Royal Navy). Born in 1922. Educated: Manchester Grammar School, and University College, Oxford. Served on a corvette as Sub. Lieutenant. His war poems appeared in a number of journals, particularly in *Penguin New Writing*.

CHRISTOPHER HASSALL (Royal Artillery, and Army Educational Corps). Born in 1912. Educated: Brighton College, and Wadham College, Oxford. Actor and lyricist before the war; first volume of poetry published in 1935. Hassall was a Staff Major at the War Office by the end of the war. After the war: author, and biographer of Stephen Haggard (q.v.), Edward Marsh, and Rupert Brooke. Died in 1964.

DESMOND HAWKINS. Born in Surrey. Novelist and editor. Farmer in Suffolk; produced the B.B.C.'s *Country Magazine*. 'Night Raid' was published in M. J. Tambimuttu's *Poetry in Wartime*, 1942.

HAMISH HENDERSON (51st Highland Division). Born 1919, in Perthshire. Henderson fought in the North African, Sicilian, and European campaigns. He wrote mostly of the bonds that, in the desert war, brought friend and foe together. His war poems were collected in 1948: also wrote songs 'some of which caught on among the troops'. With the School of Scottish Studies after the war.

RAYNER HEPPENSTALL (Royal Artillery, and R.A.P.C.). Born in 1911, at Huddersfield. Educated: Universities of Leeds and Strasbourg. Freelance writer before the war. In the Army, 1940–45. With the B.B.C. after the war. First volume of poems in 1935. 'Instead of a Carol' first appeared in *Partisan Review*.

*T. R. HODGSON (R.A.F.). Born in 1915. Thomas Rahilley Hodgson wrote poetry from the age of seventeen; most of it was collected by Routledge (*This Life, This Death*) in 1943. He was shot down and killed in May 1941.

R. C. M. HOWARD (Royal Navy). Journalist on the *Sunday Chronicle* before the war. 'The Voyage Back' was written in the Far East, in August 1945, when the author was twenty-eight. It first appeared in *Penguin New Writing* in 1947.

*JOHN JARMAIN (Royal Artillery). Jarmain fought from Alamein to Sicily, and then in the Normandy landings, as an anti-tank

gunner with the 51st Highland Division, attaining the rank of
Major. A novel, and his collected poems, were published by Collins.
He was killed by enemy mortar fire in Calvados, June 26, 1944.

*DAVID GERAINT JONES (Royal Armoured Corps). Born
in 1922, at Haverfordwest. Educated: Cheltenham, and Trinity
Hall, Cambridge. Geraint Jones was transferred from his R.A.C.
unit to the 159th Infantry Brigade H.Q., with the rank of Lieuten-
ant. He died of wounds in Normandy, June 28, 1944.

DENYS L. JONES (Army). Born in 1917. Educated: Exeter
School. Jones went to sea before the war, and then spent six years
in the Army. 'Cain in the Jungle' first appeared in *Penguin New
Writing*, in 1946.

*SIDNEY KEYES (Queen's Own Royal West Kent Regt.).
Born in 1922, at Dartford, Kent. Educated: Tonbridge, and Queen's
College, Oxford. Like Keith Douglas, and like Keyes's great friend
the poet John Heath-Stubbs, he had a difficult childhood (he was
brought up by his grandfather) and wrote considerable poetry while
still at school. In May 1942, he wrote: 'I am not a man but a voice.
My only justification is my power of speaking clearly.' He was
taken prisoner during the last days of the Tunisian campaign in
April 1943, and died in enemy hands 'of unknown causes'. He was
posthumously awarded the Hawthornden Prize.

FRANCIS KING. Born 1923, in Switzerland. Educated: Shrews-
bury, and Balliol College, Oxford. Novelist and poet. Somerset
Maugham Award, 1952. British Council Lecturer after the war. A
collection of his poems was published in 1952.

PATRICIA LEDWARD (A.T.S.). Born in 1920. Driver with
an Anti-Aircraft unit. Edited *Poems of This War*, with Colin
Strang, for Cambridge University Press, in 1942, in which the

extract in this anthology appeared. Contributor to *Poetry Quarterly*, etc.

LAURIE LEE. Born 1914, in the Cotswolds. Educated: Slad Village School, and Stroud. Travelled in Spain (Civil War) and the Mediterranean before the war. Worked on Government films, 1939–43. Ministry of Information, 1944–46. Leading poet and author.

JOHN LEHMANN. Born in 1907. Educated: Eton, and Trinity College, Cambridge. Founder-editor of *New Writing* and *The London Magazine*. Publisher, poet and author. Probably the most important and influential editor of the war years.

REGINALD LEVY (R.A.P.C.). Born in 1914, at Spitalfields, London. Educated: East End Schools. Levy was an office worker before the war. He joined the Pay Corps as a Private, and was promoted Sergeant in India. The poem by which he is represented here appeared in *Poems From India*, 1946, edited by R. N. Currey and R. V. Gibson.

*ALUN LEWIS (South Wales Borderers). Born 1915, at Aberdare. Educated: Cowbridge Grammar School, and University College, Aberystwyth. Schoolteacher before the war. Wrote some outstanding short stories of the war as well as poetry, notably 'Ward O (3)B'. Entered the Army as a Sapper in the Royal Engineers, in 1940, but was commissioned in the infantry, and went to India in 1943. He was killed accidentally by his own revolver on March 5, 1944, on the Arakan front.

JACK LINDSAY (Royal Signals). Born in 1900, at Melbourne, Australia. Brother of novelist Philip Lindsay. Educated: University of Brisbane. Settled in Essex. Prolific author, poet, classicist, novelist, and man of letters. 'Squadding' was in *New Lyrical Ballads*, 1945.

MAURICE LINDSAY (Cameronians). Born 1918, in Glasgow. Educated: Glasgow Academy, and Scottish National Academy of Music. Editor of *Poetry Scotland*. 'NAAFI Concert' was in *Sailing Tomorrow's Seas*, 1944. Journalist, author, and television executive after the war. Has had five volumes of poetry published.

LAWRENCE LITTLE (Royal Signals). Born in 1921. Educated: Alleyn's School. Lawrence Little was employed in the Office of Works before the war. Served in Africa. Contributor to the leading periodicals, including *Bugle Blast*, *New Verse* and *Penguin New Writing*; 'After Several Years' was first published in the latter in 1943. Novelist.

EMANUEL LITVINOFF (Pioneer Corps). Born 1915, in East London. Litvinoff joined the Army as Private early in the war, and was later commissioned. Two volumes of his poetry were published during the war. 'Thoughts on the Eve' was in *Poems of This War*, 1942. Journalist, television playwright.

LOUIS MACNEICE. Born in 1907, at Belfast, son of a Bishop. Educated: Marlborough, and Merton College, Oxford. University lecturer in Greek and Classics before the war. At Cornell University, United States, at the start of the war, but returned to work with the B.B.C., with which he remained for many years. Died in 1963.

H. B. MALLALIEU (Royal Artillery). Born 1914, in New Jersey, United States. Worked as a London journalist before the war. Commissioned in an L.A.A. unit, Mallalieu served in the Mediterranean and Italian theatres. Contributor of poetry to the leading publications from the late 1930s.

JOHN MANIFOLD (Intelligence Corps). Born 1915, in Melbourne. Educated: Geelong Grammar School, and Jesus College, Cambridge. Worked in Germany with a publishing house before the war. Served in several theatres including the Middle East, West Africa, and France. Manifold's war poetry was collected in 1948. 'The Recruit' appeared in *Poems from the Forces*, 1941.

GEOFFREY MATTHEWS (Royal Signals). Born 1920, in London. Educated: Kingswood, and Corpus Christi, Oxford. Published in *Horizon, Our Time, Modern Reading, The Mint*, etc. After the war: university lecturer.

FRANCES MAYO. 'Lament' was first published in *New Lyrical Ballads* in 1945: edited by Maurice Carpenter, Jack Lindsay and Honor Arundel.

KENNETH NEAL. 'Army' was published in *Poems of This War*, Cambridge University Press, in 1942.

HUBERT NICHOLSON. Born in 1908, at Hull. Journalist in the provinces before the war. Novelist. With Reuters after the war. A volume of Hubert Nicholson's war poems was published in 1943.

NORMAN NICHOLSON. Born 1914, in Cumberland. Educated at local schools. Teacher in his native county; became an established poet during the war. His verse play, *The Old Man of the Mountains*, was first produced at the Mermaid Theatre, London, just after the war. First collection of poetry published in 1944.

WILLIAM PLOMER. Born in 1903, at Pietersburg, South Africa. Educated: Rugby. Farmer in South Africa before the war, when not travelling. A selection of his early poetry was published in 1940. Plomer served at the Admiralty, 1940–45. Author.

ALEX POTTER. Born 1891, in Norwich. Infantry officer in First World War: wounded twice. On editorial staff of *Continental Daily Mail* for twenty-eight years. Interned in Second World War for four years. Collected *Verses By British Internees* in Saint-Denis camp in 1942. The entire edition of 3,000 was sold in the camp in two hours, profits going to the French Red Cross.

ENOCH POWELL (Royal Warwickshire Regiment). Born in
1912. Educated: King Edward's, Birmingham, and Trinity College,
Cambridge. Professor of Greek before the war. Rose from Private
to Brigadier. M.B.E. for services in the war, 1943. On General
Staff. M.P. for Wolverhampton S.W. since 1950. Minister of
Health, 1960–63. Two volumes of poetry published before the war,
and one volume containing war poetry in 1951.

F. T. PRINCE (Intelligence Corps). Born in 1912, at Kimberley,
South Africa. Educated at Balliol College, Oxford, and Princeton,
United States. In America before the war. His first volume of
poetry was published in 1937. Prince served in North Africa and
other theatres, and became a Captain. University lecturer after the
war. The well-anthologised 'Soldiers Bathing' first appeared in
Poems from the Forces.

JOHN PUDNEY (R.A.F.). Born in 1909. Educated: Gresham's
School. B.B.C. producer, and journalist, before the war. R.A.F.
Intelligence Officer and Public Relations; served in Africa, Mediter-
ranean, France; Squadron Leader. 'For Johnny' was written on the
back of an envelope during a London air-raid in 1941. Wrote an
official history of the Battle of Malta. Publisher after the war.

*DAVID RAIKES (R.A.F.). Born in 1924, at Blechingley,
Surrey. Educated: Radley, and Trinity College, Oxford. In crew
which won the Oxford Senior Eights, 1942. Bomber pilot in Middle
East and Italy. Raikes was reported missing from operations over
the Po Valley, April 21, 1945. His poetry was collected in 1954.

T. W. RAMSEY. This poet's first collections were in 1934 and
1935. He later published two more volumes of poetry: *Endymion to
Silver*, 1944, and *Fire and Ice*, 1946. 'Eighth Army' was published
in *Poems of the War Years*, edited by Maurice Wollman, in 1948.
President of the Poetry Society after the war.

ARNOLD RATTENBURY. 'Calendar Song' was published in *New Lyrical Ballads*, in 1945.

DEREK B. READE (South Staffordshire Regiment and Sierra Leone Regiment). Born in 1915. 'In Praise of Home and Rough Weather' was first published in the *Poetry Review*, in 1942, when the author was a Lieutenant serving in West Africa. Businessman.

HENRY REED (R.A.O.C.). Born in 1914, at Birmingham. Educated: King Edward VI School, Aston, and Birmingham University. Free-lance journalist and writer before the war. Called up in the Army, 1941, but released the following year to work at the Foreign Office. A collection of poetry was published in 1946. Radio writer after the war.

KEIDRYCH RHYS (London Welsh Regiment). Born in 1915, at Llandilo. Educated: Llandovery Grammar School. Founder-editor of *Wales*, and farmer, before the war. With anti-aircraft unit during Battle of Britain, near Dover, and later at Scapa. Editor of two popular wartime anthologies. A volume of his poetry was published in 1941. War correspondent. Journalist after the war.

ANNE RIDLER. Born in 1912, at Rugby, where her father was a master at the school. Educated: King's College, London, and Italy. Married in 1938; four children. Wrote two verse plays during the war, as well as many poems on personal and religious themes. A collection containing war poetry was published in 1943; five other collections.

MICHAEL RIVIERE (Sherwood Rangers). Born 1919, in Norwich. Educated: Magdalen College, Oxford, where he contributed to the *Oxford Magazine*. Taken prisoner in the Crete campaign, June 1941. Riviere escaped twice from prison camps, and was finally sent to the notorious 'escapers' camp', *Oflag IVC*, where he wrote the poem reproduced here. It was first published in

Penguin New Writing, 1945, and anthologised in *Poems From New Writing* the following year.

ALAN ROOK (Royal Artillery). Born in 1909. Educated: Uppingham and Oxford. Rook was at Dunkirk, became a Staff Officer, and rose to the rank of Major while still in his twenties. With the 6th A.A. Division. He was later invalided out. Editor of the Oxford magazine *Kingdom Come* with Henry Treece. Contributor to many periodicals, and three volumes containing war poetry were published. After the war: in business in Nottingham.

ALAN ROSS (Royal Navy). Born in 1922. Educated: Haileybury, and St John's College, Oxford. Played against Cambridge in cricket and squash. Served as seaman in the Arctic and North Seas; Intelligence Officer with destroyer flotillas; Naval Staff, Western Germany, 1945–46. After the war: British Council and then journalism. Editor of *London Magazine*, publisher, and cricket correspondent.

PATRICK SAVAGE (South Staffordshire Regt.). Born in 1916. Educated: Westminster and Christ Church, Oxford. Prisoner-of-war 1941–45, mostly at Eichstatt camp. A selection of Patrick Savage's poetry was published in *Home Is The Soldier*, 1947. After the war: headmaster.

DOROTHY L. SAYERS. Born in 1893. Educated: Somerville College, Oxford. Married in 1926. Author of detective stories, works on Dante, and plays and books on religious subjects. 'The English War' was first published in *The Times Literary Supplement*, 1941, but is uncollected. It was reproduced in the *The Best Poems of 1941*. Died in 1959.

VERNON SCANNELL (Gordon Highlanders). Born in 1922. Educated: Queen's Park School, Aylesbury, and Leeds University.

Won Northern Universities Boxing Championships at three weights. Served in the 51st Highland Division from Alamein to Tunis, in the invasion of Sicily, and in Normandy. Poet, novelist and critic.

FRANCIS SCARFE (R.A.O.C., and Army Educational Corps). Born in 1911. Educated: Durham University, and Fitzwilliam House, Cambridge. University lecturer before the war. Served in the Orkneys and Faroes, and reached the rank of Lt.-Colonel. Returned to university teaching in Scotland after the war. Director of British Institute in Paris.

PAUL SCOTT (The Buffs). Born 1920, in London. In account-ancy before the war. Wrote 'I, Gerontius', a well-known poem of the day, on joining the army. A selection of his war poems was published in a *Resurgam* broadsheet. Served in India. Literary agent after the war. Novelist.

IAN SERRAILLIER. Born 1912, in London. Educated: Brighton College, and St Edmund Hall, Oxford. Schoolmaster, and children's writer. 'The New Learning' appeared in *Poems of This War*, 1942.

EDITH SITWELL. Born at Scarborough, sister of Sir Osbert and Sacheverell. Author, poet, editor, and friend of poets. D.B.E., 1954. The Second War was one of her major sources of inspiration. Died in 1964.

MARTYN SKINNER. Born in 1906. His 'Letters to Malaya' were written during the war in several volumes to a friend in the Malayan Civil Service. Farmer during the war. Writer on the Arthurian legend. Hawthornden Prize, 1943.

*RICHARD SPENDER (Parachute Regiment). Born in 1921, at Hereford. Educated: King Edward VI School, Stratford-on-Avon. Spender won a scholarship to Oxford in 1940, but enlisted aged nineteen. London Irish Regt., 2nd Lieutenant; transferred to 2nd Battalion, The Parachute Regt. Killed in action, March 28, 1943, while leading his men against German machine-gun positions near Bizerta, Tunisia. Two volumes of his poetry were published. His best-known poem was probably 'Parachute Battalion', first published in *The Times Literary Supplement*.

STEPHEN SPENDER (N.F.S.). Born in 1909. Educated: University College School, and University College, Oxford. In Spain during the Civil War. In the National Fire Service, 1941–44, and then worked with the Foreign Office. Eminent poet and editor. Consultant in Poetry, Library of Congress, Washington.

DEREK STANFORD (N.C.C.). Born 1918, in Middlesex. Educated: Latymer Upper. His first collection of war and other poems was in collaboration with John Bayliss. Lecturer and critic after the war, with works on Christopher Fry, Dylan Thomas, John Betjeman, etc.

*GERVASE STEWART (Fleet Air Arm). Born in 1920. Educated: St Catharine's College, Cambridge. Editor of *Granta*, and Chairman of the Union (wartime equivalent of President). A friend of Henry Treece, Stewart was a pilot in the Fleet Air Arm, and was killed in action on August 25, 1941. *No Weed Death*, his collected poems, was published in 1942.

W. F. M. STEWART (Royal Artillery). Born in 1918, at Crieff, Perthshire. Educated: Morrison's Academy, and Edinburgh University. Gunner, Field Regt., R.A.; later commissioned. His 'Poem' first appeared in *Penguin New Writing*, in 1942.

GORDON SWAINE (Royal Artillery). Born in 1920, in Malaya. Educated: Blundell's and Jesus College, Oxford. Served in North Africa and Italy; Captain, 22 L.A.A. Regt. After the war: publishing and advertising.

GORDON SYMES (Intelligence Corps). Born 1917, in Shropshire. Educated: Worcester College, Oxford. He was first in infantry, but transferred to Intelligence. Served in France, 1940; India, 1943–44; United States, 1945. Contributed to many periodicals.

JULIAN SYMONS (Royal Armoured Corps). Born 1912, in London. Company secretary before the war, and editor of *Twentieth Century Verse*. In the Army, 1942–44; invalided out. Biographer, historian and writer of crime novels.

GEORGE TAYLOR (R.A.F.). Born 1914, at St Leonard's-on-Sea, in Sussex, where he worked in local government. Began writing poetry while serving in India, and was represented in *Poems From India*, 1946, as were James K. Cassels and H. H. Tilley. After the war: educational administration at Oxford University and in Sussex.

A. S. J. TESSIMOND. Born in 1902. Educated: Liverpool University. An advertising copywriter in London during the 1930s. His early poetry was published before the war. 'England' first appeared in *Penguin New Writing* in 1941.

DYLAN THOMAS Born in 1914, at Swansea. Educated: Swansea Grammar School. Reviewer and free-lance journalist before the war. Rejected by the Army, he wrote propaganda film-scripts during the war. Notable poet, radio writer and reader. Died in 1953.

*FRANK THOMPSON (Royal Artillery, and Special Duties). Born 1920, at Darjeeling, son of the First World War poet Edward Thompson. Educated: Winchester, and New College, Oxford. Fought in the Desert Campaign, and Sicily landings. Major with G.H.Q. Liaison (Phantom) Regt. Then parachuted into South Serbia to help the Bulgarian Partisan Army. Surrounded with a small force, captured, and 'executed' publicly; aged twenty-three. Poetry and letters published by Gollancz in 1947.

TERENCE TILLER. Born 1916, in Cornwall. Educated: Jesus
College, Cambridge. University lecturer before the war. In Cairo,
1939–46. Contributor of poetry to many publications. Two volumes
of poetry published in the war. Worked with the B.B.C. after the
war.

H. H. TILLEY (Army Educational Corps). Born in 1910. Edu-
cated: Halesowen Grammar School, Worcester, and Birmingham
University. Teacher and journalist before the war. Royal Signals
but transferred to A.E.C. in 1941. Served in India.

RUTHVEN TODD. Born in 1914, at Edinburgh. Educated:
Fettes, and Edinburgh College of Art. Art critic, prolific author,
poet and lecturer. 'These Are Facts' was anthologised by Julian
Symons in *An Anthology of War Poetry*, 1942.

JOHN R. TOWNSEND (R.A.F.). Educated at Leeds Gram-
mar School. Served in Middle East and Italy. 'Poem After Victory'
was first published in *Penguin New Writing* in 1947. After the war:
Cambridge, journalist, and children's writer.

HENRY TREECE (R.A.F.). Born in 1912, at Wednesbury,
Staffs. Educated: local High School, and Birmingham University
where he was captain of boxing. Schoolmaster before the war. A
leader of the New Apocalyptic movement of 1939 and the early
1940s. R.A.F. Intelligence, 1941–46. Editor of *Wartime Harvest*,
etc. Novelist, poet and teacher.

G. A. WAGNER (Welsh Guards). Born in 1927. Educated:
Christ Church, Oxford, and Columbia University. Wounded in the
Middle East. Published war poetry in several publications. Became
a university lecturer in New York after the war. Novelist.

JAMES WALKER (R.A.F.). Born 1911, in Manchester. Spent
childhood on the fairground. Educated: secondary school in North
Wales. Poet, playwright, novelist, critic, and broadcaster.

JOHN WALLER (R.A.S.C.). Born in 1917, at Oxford. Educated: Weymouth College, and Worcester College, Oxford. Founder-editor of *Kingdom Come*. 'Aldershot' first appeared in *Horizon*. John Waller served in the Middle East, 1941–46, for much of the time attached to the Ministry of Information. Editor, with Erik de Mauny, of *Middle East Anthology*, 1946. Succeeded to a baronetcy in 1954. Journalist, teacher, and author.

JOHN WEDGE (Royal Navy). Born 1921, in London. Educated: Roan School. Served in the North Sea, Atlantic and Channel, starting as a telegraphist and finishing as Lieutenant. Bank manager after the war.

*NIGEL WEIR (R.A.F.). Born in 1919, the son of the founder of the famous pre-war Oxford University Air Squadron. Educated: Winchester, and Christ Church, Oxford. Fencing half-Blue. Weir fought in the Battle of Britain, and destroyed three enemy planes during the Blitz on August 8, 1940. Awarded the D.F.C. Killed in action, November 1940. Poetry collected by Faber, 1941.

DENTON WELCH. Born in 1915, at Shanghai. Educated: Repton, from which he ran away at sixteen, and the Goldsmiths' School of Art, London. Talented artist, short-story writer, and poet. Knocked off his bicycle by a motorist in June 1935, and received severe spinal injuries. His health never fully recovered, and he died in December 1948.

L. J. YATES (Army). Born in 1918. L. J. Yates was a clerk before the war. He served with the B.E.F., was at Dunkirk, and was later posted to the Middle East. 'Soldier' was first printed in *New Writing and Daylight*, 1942.

Some published poets

who died on active service 1939-45

Drummond Allison (East Surrey Regt.)
Brian Allwood (R.A.F.)
J. P. Angold (R.A.F.)
Cameron Bailey (K.R.R.C.)
A. D. Bass (R.A.M.C.)
J. R. Blythe (Merchant Navy)
J. F. Boughey (Coldstream Guards)
David Bourne (R.A.F.)
Clive Branson (R.A.C.)
O. O. Breakwell (Coldstream Guards)
O. C. Chave (R.A.F.)
M. Chevenix Trench (R.E.)
Timothy Corsellis (R.A.F.)
Keith Douglas (Sherwood Rangers)
F. R. Dunton (R.A.F.)
Keith Foottit (R.A.F.)
David Graves (R. Welch Fusiliers)
Stephen Haggard (Intelligence Corps)
T. R. Hodgson (R.A.F.)
John Jarmain (R.A.)
Robert Joly (Grenadier Guards)
D. R. Geraint Jones (R.A.C.)
Sidney Keyes (Queen's Own R. West Kent Regt.)
Alun Lewis (South Wales Borderers)
Sorley MacLean
John MacLeish (King's Own R. Regt.)
J. D. Maclure (Royal Scots)
M. Macnaughton-Smith (R.A.F.)
H. N. T. Medrington (R.A.F.)

I. O. Meikle (R.A.)
T. A. Mellows (7th Lancers)
David Raikes (R.A.F.)
William Rose (Royal Navy)
R. Brian Scott (Army)
Richard Spender (Parachute Regt.)
Gervase Stewart (Fleet Air Arm)
R. D. D. Thomas (Grenadier Guards)
Frank Thompson (R.A.)
Andrew Tod (R. Scots Fusiliers)
Bertram Warr (R.A.F.)
Nigel Weir (R.A.F.)
Jonathan Wilson (Scots Guards)

INDEX

Page references to poems are shown in italic

Also available in Methuen Paperbacks

An anthology selected by Brian Gardner

UP THE LINE TO DEATH

Before his death on active service in 1918 Wilfred Owen
had written, 'Above all I am not concerned with Poetry.
My subject is War and the pity of War.' This anthology,
too, is concerned more with the First World War than
with poetry; it is not only a collection, but a book with a
theme. Seventy-two poets are represented, of whom
twenty-one died in action.

Kipling, Brooke, Sassoon, Blunden, Owen are all here,
as well as poets almost entirely forgotten now. From the
early exultation to the bitter disillusion, the tragedy of the
First World War is carefully traced in the words of those
who lived through it.

'Mr Brian Gardner, who has chosen, introduced and put
notes to this admirable anthology, shows the First
World War poets in all moods.'   *The Times*

'To read through this anthology ... is to live the years
1914–18, adding to the images of battle which most of us
have already the actual feelings expressed by the soldier
poets who lived, and died, through trench warfare.'
                        The Times Educational Supplement

also available in Magnum

These and other Magnum Books are available at your bookshop or newsagent. In case of difficulty orders may be sent to:

Magnum Books
Cash Sales Department
P.O. Box 11
Falmouth
Cornwall TR10 10QEN

Please send cheque or postal order, no currency, for purchase price quoted and allow the following for postage and packing:

UK: 19p for the first book plus 9p per copy for each additional book up to a maximum of 73p.

BFPO & Eire: 19p for the first book plus 9p per copy for the next six books, thereafter 3p per book.

Other Overseas Customers: 20p for the first book plus 10p per copy for each additional book.

While every effort is made to keep prices low, it is sometimes necessary to increase prices at short notice. Magnum Books reserve the right to show new retail prices on covers which may differ from those previously advertised in the text or elsewhere.